5 C HERO

The Joel Stephens Story

Michael G. D'Aloisio

authorHOUSE®

AuthorHouse™
1663 Liberty Drive
Bloomington, IN 47403
www.authorhouse.com
Phone: 1-800-839-8640

First published by AuthorHouse 12/1/2009

ISBN: 978-1-4490-5420-5 (e)
ISBN: 978-1-4490-5418-2 (sc)
ISBN: 978-1-4490-5419-9 (hc)

Library of Congress Control Number: 2009912483

Printed in the United States of America
Bloomington, Indiana

This book is printed on acid-free paper.

Contents

Part I

Part II

Part III

Dedicated to

Joel Stephens

1976-1998

On September 30, 1998, the Baltimore Orioles lost a member of their family in minor league player Joel Stephens. Joel was a very unique and special young man. The way that he led his life and the courage and faith that he displayed were lessons to all of us. We only wish that everyone could have been touched by Joel and could have experienced him the way that we did. Joel's memory will live on with the Orioles family forever.

Dedication

To the memory of the three most important people in my life who have left this world and who have served as my inspiration – my mom, Josephine T. D'Aloisio, my dad, Michael V. D'Aloisio, and my friend, Joel Andrew Stephens. Thank you for teaching me to believe in myself, laugh, think, pray, dream, and to enjoy life today with family and friends.

To Ron and Joyce Stephens, and to the entire Stephens family, your love and faith is an example for us all.

Acknowledgements

I want to thank Tony Pucci for his support and help in the writing of this book. Without your encouragement and your faithful friendship, the story of Joel Stephens could have never been completed and passed on from one generation to the next. Thank you for keeping me motivated and focused, and for always being there when I needed a friend.

I want to express my gratitude to the coaches and athletes with whom I have had the pleasure to associate over the past thirty years. Your friendships and the memories we shared have been valuable assets to Jayne and me. In some small way, I hope that I have had a small and positive impact on your lives because you have all had such a huge impact on mine. It is these memories that will forever keep you close to my heart.

I am grateful to Fr. Vincent McDonough and to my mother-in-law, Mary Lou Tremaine, for guiding me and helping me to think about what is important in the world, and encouraging me always by their example.

I am sincerely grateful to the Elmira *Star Gazette* sports editor Andrew Legare, and *Washington Post* sports writer, Barry Svrluga, formerly of the *Corning Leader*, for their professionalism and for their help in providing information for this book.

Although I cannot mention every person by name because of the chance of omitting someone, I want to express my deepest appreciation to the hundreds who sent me sympathy cards and letters after Joel's death. Never to be forgotten, you helped me through a very difficult time and I am forever grateful.

Finally, I want to thank the person who has listened to me read this book out loud a hundred times, and tell the story of Joel ten times as many - my wife, Jayne. I value and respect your opinion. You are my love, my best friend, and my soul mate. Through the difficult times, you have always been at my side for support. My devotion for you continues to grow with every passing day. Without your love and encouragement, I never would have the quality in my life that I continue to share with you each and every day. Thank you for being my pillar.

Foreword

Even though Joel Stephens lived only twenty-two short years, he had a lasting impact on the people who knew him or knew of him. As a coach since 1975, I have been blessed to know a number of players who have had a profound impact on my own life, and whom I consider true champions. A champion is not just someone who is a winner in sports. A champion is also someone who fights for a cause such as civil rights or freedom. To me, Joel Stephens was a champion not because of his athletic ability, but rather because of his unrelenting belief that his faith would serve as an example for us to follow. General George S. Patton once said, "If a man does his best, what else is there?"

In his Inaugural Address in 2009, President Barack Obama expressed his belief that "There is nothing so satisfying to the spirit, so defining of our character, than giving our all to a difficult task." The true measure of a champion is the person who has faith at the most challenging of times and whose positive outlook and best effort always remains paramount in life.

In the eight years that we were friends, I realized that there was so much more to Joel than just a talented athlete. Upon his death in September of 1998, I felt a gap had been created in my life. I realized that the only way to fill that gap was to inform people about Joel Stephens and to tell his story. Joel believed that the length of a person's time on earth did not determine its quality. Rather, it was how you thought and acted towards others that determined the value of one's life. That was my reason for creating the Joel Andrew Stephens 5 C Award which is bestowed yearly on the Twin Tiers top football player / humanitarian. It is also awarded annually at Notre Dame High School to an athlete / citizen to recognize the positive contributions that they have made throughout their careers. In both awards, the recipients must possess the same qualities that made Joel Stephens a champion – the 5 Cs – Christianity, Courage, Character, Compassion, and Commitment.

Now, as we approach the eleventh anniversary of his death, I want to share the story of the Joel Stephens I knew.

September 12, 2009
Elmira, New York

Chapter 1

An Everyday Angel

Elmira is a small blue collar town in upstate New York. It is located six miles from the Pennsylvania border, having a population of 33,000. Known primarily for housing some of the state's most disreputable criminals in one of its two maximum security prisons, it has been the birthplace or home to many notable celebrities. Included on this list are the likes of Ernie Davis (first African-American to win the Heisman Award), Tommy Hilfiger (fashion designer), Brian Williams (anchor, *NBC Nightly News*), Eileen Collins (first female to command the space shuttle), Frank Gannett (founder of the Gannett newspaper chain), Duke Carroll (National Football League official), and Samuel Clemens, who wrote under the pen name, Mark Twain. All of these people have had a profound and positive effect on our community and the surrounding area. However, if you talk to the people of the Southern Tier of New York and the Northern Tier of Pennsylvania, one prominent name is noticeably missing. It is the name of a high school sports legend and a goodwill ambassador who also had a major impact on the lives of these same people in our towns. This person's name is Joel Andrew Stephens. To many of us, regardless of age, Joel Stephens was an "Everyday Angel" on temporary loan from a much higher venue. Even though people who knew him or knew of him, thought of him this way, he was too humble and modest to ever accept this accolade.

Joel Stephens was born in Tioga, Pennsylvania on March 15, 1976 where he did chores and honed his athletic skills on the 100-acre family farm and farmhouse that his dad and grandfathers built in 1975. This prodigy was diagnosed with a rare form of colon cancer in the fall of 1997. Despite his courageous and valiant battle, this disease eventually took his life on September 30, 1998. Joel Stephens was a soft-spoken, gentle person who had an abundance of charisma and sincerity, all of which transcended racial, religious, and socio-economic differences. Joel Stephens grew up as a Pentecostal Christian, but attended a Roman Catholic high school on the Southside of Elmira. He regularly stopped to visit various churches, synagogues, shrines, and memorials during his much too short twenty-two years. He felt comfortable and at ease, paying homage and respect in having conversations with his Maker, no matter what the time or day. Joel was once asked what religion he practiced, and he responded, "Does it really matter? We all pray to the same God." When he passed away, a highly successful Jewish doctor, as well as a local Jewish sportscaster, both of whom followed Joel's high school career, brought to my attention that that day was the feast of Yom Kippur, the most sacred of all Jewish holidays. It is widely believed by the Jewish faith community that only the holiest of all are ever taken from this earth on this revered day. It is ironic and fitting, perhaps even prophetic, that this remarkable individual went to his final home and resting place on this most blessed day.

Chapter 2

The Early Years

From early on in his quest to become a not so ordinary athlete, young Joel took up the sport of wrestling with Jim Smalley as his coach at R.B. Elementary School in Williamson, Pennsylvania. For his skills, determination, sportsmanship, and for making quick work of his competition, he was often named most outstanding wrestler in meets that featured participants as old as 12. As a 10-year-old, weighing 75 pounds and representing the Warriors Wrestling Club of Tioga, Pennsylvania, Joel won the Midget U.S. Federation State Championship held at Penn State University. He was the first state champion out of this organization that is located in the hotbed of Pennsylvania wrestling. After this experience, Joel went on to compete in the Middle Atlantic American Athletic Union Championships in Richmond, Virginia where once again he dominated the competition. After a grueling, hectic, and rigorous schedule, Joel traveled back north to Easton, Pennsylvania where he placed second in his division out of 1,187 wrestlers in the National Junior Olympics held at Lafayette College in 1986.

In Kansas City, with 37 states having their respective champions competing for titles, Joel as a twelve-year-old, represented Pennsylvania in the 100-pound weight division where he earned a silver medal in a hard-fought one-point loss to a boy from Oklahoma. He continued to wrestle through his eighth grade, winning many Freestyle, Greco-Roman, and Grand National Wrestling Championship Tournaments throughout the country. His final overall wrestling record was 423 wins and 29 losses. Some of Joel's other accomplishments included winning the USA Wrestling Federation State Championship for three consecutive years, winning the AAU Eastern Folk Style State Championship, capturing the Eastern National Freestyle Championship, as well as winning the AAU Eastern National Freestyle and Greco-Roman Championships.

Despite his many successes in wrestling, the young Joel Stephens wanted to pursue his newly acquired taste for football and baseball, playing them both tirelessly at the local parks and ball fields. An avid New York Yankees and Dallas Cowboys fan, he asked his dad to build a batting cage in their basement so that he could hit balls off a tee long into the night. Even at this young age, he somewhat resembled his two favorite pro athletes, Troy Aikman and Mickey Mantle, to whom later he would be compared by an elderly baseball scout for the Minnesota Twins. Joel also saved some money and again with his parents' help and support, purchased a set of free-style weights so that he could begin a lifting regimen.

Chapter 3

Pre – Notre Dame Period

It was January 1991 and Elmira Notre Dame High School was still riding high coming off a New York State Football Championship the prior year. The school's administration had their annual Open House scheduled for prospective students and parents contemplating a Catholic education. Many have viewed Notre Dame High School as a religious based, college preparatory establishment where parents could invest in their child's future. This center for higher education is a place of learning that tries to affably blend faith, academics, athletics, and life into a culture where students try to achieve their maximum potential. The importance of challenging students spiritually, academically, emotionally, athletically, and physically was something that the Stephens family had been seriously discussing for some time. The Stephens clan had roots planted firmly in Christianity. A religious education was a primary reason for them venturing into the possibility of private institutions. Ron Stephens had been a member of the Tioga School Board for a few years and he was beginning to inquire about parochial schools in the Elmira, Williamsport, and Corning areas that put a greater emphasis on preparation for higher education.

In checking with some Notre Dame alumni, the Stephens family found that this co-ed school operated by the Sisters of Mercy put a great deal of importance on faith, compassion, respect, self worth, social justice, and service to others. They welcomed the idea of a school and the families working in a close partnership to foster Christian values and academic excellence. The Stephens family believed that the more you gave to others, the more you got to keep for yourself. After listening to the Sisters and the Guidance Department's enrollment presentation, people in attendance were given a guided tour of the school after which they could meet with individual teachers and administrators to ask specific questions. It was apparent that Ron Stephens knew I was the football and basketball coach as he approached me, asking if I might answer some questions. His son was beginning high school in the fall and was considering attending Williamson High School, in a district in which his mother was a teacher. This small school system is located in Pennsylvania just a few miles below the hill from the Stephens home. Joel had acquired an eager interest, and new enthusiasm for playing football, basketball, and baseball, and possibly trying to earn a scholarship to college. Although Williamson High School had basketball, wrestling, and baseball teams, they did not offer a scholastic football program. Ron was somewhat sold on the idea of sending his son to our school, even though the tuition and commute of 35 miles would be a burden at times. He felt comfortable that his son would be in a safe, positive, and supportive climate that encouraged the students to become active agents in their own education and development. He liked the idea of the Notre Dame faculty, staff, and coaches being an extended family. He also liked the opportunity for his son to become a member of a fairly successful high school football program.

After a 20-minute friendly conversation, we shook hands and wished each other luck. It was the first time I had ever met Ron Stephens or heard of his family. There was just something about his candor and openness that made me comfortable, and gave me a feeling that I had known him all of my life. While walking back to my office, I was quickly approached by our head wrestling coach, Steve Weber. He wanted to know if the gentleman that I just had been conversing with was Mr. Stephens from Tioga, and I replied that it was. Steve alluded to the fact that the gentlemen's son was one of the most skilled wrestlers on the East coast, and that he surely hoped that the family would enroll their son at their earliest convenience. Also, Steve hoped that I did not say anything that would sway their decision, possibly sending Joel to wrestle for a rival school. It did strike me as strange that Ron Stephens never mentioned his son was a wrestler, nor a three-time Pennsylvania State Champion. I came to realize that this modesty and humbleness handed down from grandfather to father and from father to son was a benchmark of the family. I remember that I muttered to my fellow coaching colleague that the father omitted that Joel was a wrestler, but he did state that his son thoroughly enjoyed playing football, basketball, and baseball.

Chapter 4

Freshman Year

Joel Stephens entered Notre Dame High School without any fanfare, marching bands, trumpet blasts, or elaborate hoopla. Nobody knew of his previous successes, prior accolades, who he was, or what he was all about. He attended our school with two wrestling friends who had just recently transferred from Cowanesque Valley High School, Dan and Kevin Wilson. This made for an easier trek in their daily car pooling trips, keeping each other alert during their rides to and from school, games, and late night practices. They also talked about teachers, coaches, incidents during the day, and I am sure maybe not always in a positive vein, about me. One of my duties as Assistant Principal is to be in charge of discipline and they knew that tardiness to homeroom was frowned upon.

One morning, Steve Weber and I made a trip to the boys' former grammar school on a not so pleasant day. They had some fairly new wrestling mats that were for sale and anything was better than the dried out, torn, concrete-like pads that we had been using. Our trip took us a little over an hour each way, all the time, carefully trying to navigate through winding roads, blind corners, narrow pavement, and inclement weather, which seemed to be the norm most of the time. I recall saying to Steve when we returned, that I would step back from pressing those boys again for arriving to school each morning a few minutes late. Forcing them to move at a faster pace and possibly causing a senseless accident was not really something that I needed on my conscience. I also had a new-found respect for these boys and their families, and for

8

the sacrifices they were making to send them to an academic institution some forty miles away.

Football had started in mid-August for both the varsity and JV teams, and Joel and a player named Mike Jeronimo began a friendly, yet very competitive, spirited rivalry. Mike was another good looking, solidly built player who was born on a Jamaican commune sixteen years earlier. Both players were quick, strong, intelligent, and they made an immediate impression on the coaching staff at both levels. When I say that they were intelligent, I mean that they had classroom smarts as well as a football IQ that was well ahead of their years. However, there were some differences between the two. Mike was neither motivated, nor was he as hardworking or as big as Joel. Maybe because of his tough childhood, Mike seemed to have a chip on his shoulder, daring anyone to knock it off. There was always great respect shown to each other and Joel became Mike's best friend. That was not anything out of the ordinary. People gravitated towards Joel because he was easy to talk with, and he never made value judgments of anyone.

Three games into the season, I decided to work individually with the junior varsity running backs before and after the varsity's practice for 20 minutes per session. I felt that Joel and Mike Jeronimo could benefit from some extra time, working on stances, starts, meshes, and steps. Three more weeks had passed and I felt that Joel, even though just a freshman, was ready physically for the rigors of varsity competition. He made his varsity debut against Susquehanna Valley, a larger school in the Binghamton area. As usual, coaches cannot make everyone happy and I knew that starting a freshman in place of a senior would draw the ire of a certain family, and maybe even a few. I reasoned that if we advance students in the classroom because they have more ability, then it was only logical to do the same in my classroom, the football field.

Joel's eyes were as big as headlights; those big steel blues were just anxious to get it on. Was Joel scared? Was he questioning this move up in competition and ability levels? No, Joel was ready, he was focused, and he would not disappoint in this unveiling. It was Saturday morning, November 2, 1991 and the bright yellow school bus was rumbling down Route 17 on its way to the Binghamton area. Sitting in the second row from the front was this freshman, interacting with the juniors and seniors scattered throughout. He was just a few hours from his first varsity game as a starter. Having been at Notre Dame for only two months, there still may have been players on the bus wondering who he was. Going over play after play of the more complicated varsity system, he was ready and eager for the contest to begin. It was a cold day and his number 89 at the time did not even appear in the game's program. The announcer had to ask someone in the stands who he was. By the end of the contest with Notre Dame winning 25-12, he wouldn't have to ask again.

On his first carry, Joel effortlessly took the ball from the quarterback, his head and eyes up and looking for daylight, a seam, an opening. He got into the hole with cat-like quickness, broke two tackles, scurried to the sideline, pulled away from a defender, and raced 67 yards for a touchdown. There was more to come for those in attendance on that brilliant, sun-soaked, chilly fall afternoon. Joel toted the pigskin 13 times for 183 yards and 3 touchdowns. He also had touchdown runs of 46 and 77 yards called back because of procedure penalties against our team. Those penalties and loss of yardage did not concern Joel, but they perturbed me.

Our program has always prided itself on not making mental mistakes and to make two in the same game was unfathomable in my opinion. It was especially unsettling because it also cost us two touchdowns. After the game, Joel nonchalantly shook the opposing players' hands and quietly headed back to our locker room. Watching Joel practice, prepare and play made me say to myself out loud, "And they call me a perfectionist?" I also thought that we were pretty lucky as a staff because we were going to have this "Horse," one of the few nicknames I gave him, for three more years.

Chapter 5

Sophomore Year

Joel played baseball and basketball all summer in the Pennsylvania leagues, and he continued to hit the weights very hard. He also did extensive roadwork, running up and down hills in Tioga Junction, which is pretty much the landscape of the entire county. Coming into the football double sessions, he had grown to six feet and his 180-pound body began to become more defined. His legs were always thick and strong. These tree stump look-alikes would make the opposition cringe thinking that they would have to somehow corral this stallion to the ground. That was the year that he made people take notice of his desire, his abilities, and his aspirations not to be ordinary. In October of 1992, the local newspaper had an article on the five most highly regarded running backs in their circulation area. Through no fault of their own, the Elmira *Star-Gazette* did not include the sophomore from Notre Dame, but then again, Joel Stephens was not yet a household name. I knew Joel was the first back in our area to rush for over 1000 yards in his first nine games, and he was still just only half way through his sophomore campaign. Yes, these footballers were quality Division I running backs galloping up and down the sidelines, and these five mentioned in the article deserved to be in that category. However, one name was conspicuously omitted and it was apparent to the ND staff that his name should have been mentioned in the same breath as the other elite of the region. Even though only sixteen-years-old, this youngster ran like he was possessed, never losing yardage or taking a step backwards. He finished off runs with an adeptness and dexterity that was uncommon to high school football in the Elmira area. After this article hit the stands, I decided to turn Joel loose in a Friday night away game against a tough undefeated squad from Trumansburg. Trumansburg had a solid program and was state ranked going into the game, and they were a nemesis and rival in all the sports in which the two schools battled. Joel carried the brunt of the load, leading Notre Dame to a very one-sided, 35-3 victory, thus sealing a playoff spot for the Crusaders.

After Joel's first touchdown, he dropped the pigskin in the end zone and began to high five his teammates who were rushing to meet him. I quietly called him to my side and mentioned that we like to hand the ball to the officials after a score for safekeeping. This practice was initiated and popularized by Larry Csonka of the Miami Dolphins. I explained that we do not ever drop the ball unattended, nor do we ever celebrate like a five-year-old on Christmas morning, something the pro players do on routine plays. Just a simple gesture, this routine of handing the ball to the official was done as a motivational ploy, always feeling we were going to give it to one of those zebras again real soon, and we wanted the officials to take good care of it. I wanted Joel to be excited, but I also wanted him to keep it in proper perspective. Joel adopted this practice on a regular basis over the next three years, almost racing as fast to the official for the handoff as he did getting in for the score. It was in the third quarter of that game and with the game still somewhat on the line that Joel Stephens gave a glimpse of what was to come for the next two years. Facing fourth and eight at midfield, my emotions took over my better judgment and I decided to go for it. Joel took the handoff from Tom McNamara and darted right and was met by a host of defenders at the line of scrimmage, some of them trying to cut him down like a lumberjack would try to take down an oak. To the amazement of those on our sidelines, and the opponent's chain crew, Joel got the eight yards and turned it into a touchdown. It was not that he got it, but rather how he got it. Hit at the line of scrimmage, parallel to the ground, and both knees only inches from the turf, he somehow kept his stability, doing a balancing act on the tips of his toes and his right hand. With the ball in his opposite hand, he traveled eight yards in this tripod position, all the while crabbing and keeping his equilibrium. He then righted himself and blazed unscathed to the end zone. The Trumansburg people who saw this display of strength and determination just shook their heads in astonishment. It was a play that simply describing does not do justice.

Old timers who came to the Notre Dame games and who were around to remember the "Elmira Express" (Ernie Davis) often commented to me after games of the similarities between these two gentlemen. These comparisons were not just of their athletic abilities, but also of the way they conducted themselves off the fields of play. This was also echoed to me by officials who worked our game, some of whom had been teammates of the late Ernie Davis. Joel had the "it" factor. People talk about "it," but no one really knows what "it" is. They just knew Joel had "it." Joel used a blend of speed, power, balance, patience, and vision to run over and around defenders. Joel's next game was against an Olean squad who were much larger in stature, and with a greater number of players. They traveled over 100 miles to play a Friday night game under the lights at our Brewer Memorial Stadium. This was the Crusader's home field, a meticulously well-maintained gridiron, dedicated to the memory of the late Joseph Brewer. Joe was an alumni football player who was tragically killed in the Vietnam conflict in 1969. By now, word had traveled through the communities that a young tailback on the south side of the river was making waves. Once again, this sophomore phenom carried the ball, as well as the team, to a resounding 34-0 homecoming victory. It seemed that week after week, more and more spectators and scouts filled the stands, watching someone that they realized was very talented. When Joel broke into the defensive secondary, it was like sending a sledgehammer to take care of a mosquito. It was simply no contest.

The newspaper did a feature article on Joel perhaps thinking it would make amends for their snub a few weeks earlier. Joel spoke in typical Joel Stephens fashion, saying that other backs mentioned were better, and that what was important to him was that he try and do everything he could to help the team get wins. He admitted to Andrew Legare, the reporter on assignment for this job, that he hated to lose in anything in which a score was being kept. Always a competitor, Joel's boyish and humble charm won over even the staunchest and toughest naysayers and skeptics. Along with Orlando Smith, a running back from Elmira Free Academy who later starred at the University of Cincinnati, these two made every all-star team, with Joel the only sophomore member. His off season custom of practicing the 5 Ps would become part of his total makeup – "Proper Preparation Prevents Poor Performance." He incessantly worked at this to the Nth degree when it came to performing on the athletic fields. His off season work had paid big dividends, allowing this Notre Dame Crusader to rush for 1,207 yards on 175 carries, and 13 touchdowns during the 1992 campaign. These totals laid the groundwork for him to break the school's all-time rushing record in his junior year, an achievement held by Bob Grosvenor who went on to be a three year starter and star at defensive back for the Syracuse Orangemen. To Joel, it was never about the glory, or setting records. It was always all about progressing as a person and moving forward.

Even though Joel was not into statistics, his totals after two seasons gave him the opportunity to set his sights on the metro Elmira and Section IV records down the road. Individual sports records were not trophies that Joel ever shot for. On the other hand, he liked to shoot and track for other prey. Joel was an avid hunter and fisherman, and next to sports, this was a passionate love. He and his dad would get their bucks and fishing limits every year, and it never took either one of them very long.

14

The Stephens family and myself were getting closer and closer, meeting and conversing after just about every game as I left the field. I learned that Joel had two brothers and a sister. His eldest brother, Aaron, was a smaller version of Joel, only with dark hair. He had been the best athlete at Williamson High School four years earlier, playing soccer and making every all-star team as a lightning quick, point guard on the basketball team. He was then a student at Penn State University, majoring in physical therapy. Further into the school year, I met Joel's little sister, Lindsey, and his other brother, David. Lindsey later enrolled at Notre Dame and she was well liked by everyone. She had an upbeat personality, a great sense of humor, and was courted by just about every male in the school. At times, however, I felt bad for Lindsey because people often, but not consciously, referred to her as Joel Stephens' little sister.

The day after being introduced to his younger brother, David, I remember going home and thinking that I would have a question or two the next time Joel and I met. At the next practice, I bluntly put the question to him, "Did your mother remarry?" With an inquisitive look on his movie star face, Joel wondered why I would ever ask this ridiculous question. I replied that I wasn't the smartest man on the face of this earth, but if he hadn't noticed, he and David were not of the same color. "Oh, that" he responded. Joel never saw the color of a person's skin, nor cared if a person had a 150 IQ, or a 50 IQ. With the immense peripheral vision he possessed as an athlete, he had blinders on when it came to making value judgments of anyone, or seeing flaws or limitations in others. Joel explained the story of his younger brother. David was one of Joel's little wrestling partners from sixth grade who lived and was raised on the other side of the mountain, just David and his single mom, the only African-American family in town. David's dad had left three days before he was born. One day, David's mom asked if the Stephens family could watch David for a weekend. Showing up at Joel's house with a garbage bag containing all of his clothes and belongings, David's mom left, never to return from her trip that evening. Joyce Stephens had no idea that the bag held David's clothes, and she accidentally tossed it out with the household rubbish. From that day on, David received a brand new, complete wardrobe of all name brand merchandise, and never went without. More important than the tangible commodities he now had, David always felt the love and affection that his newfound family freely offered. This love was unconditional, and it was tested in David's senior year when he began running with the wrong crowd, and was charged by law enforcement during an altercation at his high school. In some unusual way, Joel felt responsible for David's error in judgment and took it upon his shoulders to turn this negative into a positive. David had enormous respect for Joel and listened to his mentoring. David eventually earned a scholarship and enrolled at Virginia Commonwealth University, getting a degree, raising a beautiful family, partly because Joel trusted and believed in him.

Chapter 6

Junior Year – Football

Joel checked in with me a few times over the summer before his junior year. He knew I was a big eater, and I often took the captains out for lunch or dinner. We always enjoyed each other's company discussing pro and college baseball, basketball, football, high school players and opponents, girl situations, who's dating who, and everything else under the sun. Joel had a terrific memory and was always up to date on just about every athlete in the country from high school on up to the big leagues. I marveled at how he could rattle off names, numbers, and statistics of everything he read. Joel was a health and fitness buff, only eating chicken or pasta, fruits, salads, and vegetables. He did not drink alcohol, soda, or smoke cigarettes. His favorite dishes were chicken parmesan, spaghetti, fettuccini alfredo, and pizza on occasion, with red meat never entering the equation. The only beverages I ever saw him drink were water or iced tea. He always ordered two glasses at a sitting.

Every fall there was a secret keg party at which many of the athletes have their one last hurrah prior to the start of the season. As usual in most high schools, some drink themselves into oblivion, and others attend this social event just for the exposure, and to share summer stories. Joel was always confident in his image but not cocky, and he felt he did not have to impress anyone by being loud, or being the center of attention in conversations. Once the beer started flowing, and with cigarettes of all kinds and shapes making an appearance, Joel knew it was time to vacate the premises. Two freshmen, who later turned out to be good athletes in their own right, began to feel very uncomfortable with what their adolescent eyes were witnessing. They knew they had to leave but without a driver's license and out in the middle of nowhere, they were locked into the scene. Joel understood people, and he understood body language. He also had a very good handle on situations and whether they were good or bad. Unbeknownst to Joel, one of these boys was my nephew, Dan Bennett. Joel, knowing the apprehensiveness of the two, approached the awkward teenagers and told them that he would take them out of there, treat them to pizza and wings, and get them home. Joel was always observant of others' feelings and he read people like a book, making it a point to be there for others. These boys did not care any more about the party, but rather were in their glory thinking to themselves that Joel Stephens would take them for eats. It wasn't until later that they realized that Joel was protecting them from a potentially regrettable evening and ending, not to mention what their parents might have done to them. While at the pizza parlor, Joel provided encouragement and direction for these impressionable youths. He further explained about the dangers of getting caught in compromising situations and how that could destroy a reputation.

As the 1993 season began, the coaching staff was not comfortable with the lack of experience, especially on our offensive line. We were coming off another championship, and we knew that it would be difficult to replace a number of all stars that had graduated. The situation was further complicated because we just didn't see much help coming from the junior varsity squad to solve our dilemma. We did have Joel coming back to attack and dissect defensives, offensives, and doing it from sideline to sideline, end zone to end zone, and everything in between. A couple of days prior to our football version of midnight madness, I was golfing with a friend whose sons were players, and who were close friends with Joel. Teeing off at the third hole of the Mark Twain Golf Course, Jack Sheehan mentioned that he was introduced to the "franchise" and that he had spent the night at his house, playing Madden football, and watching old game tapes with his sons. I innocently asked, "Who's the franchise?" Perplexed that I would ask such a dumb question, Jack said "Joel Stephens," and added that he was a great deal larger in person than he appeared to be when observing him from a distance in the stands. Joel then was a bit over 6'1" and 193 pounds, and as always, in tremendous physical condition. At our last coaching meeting, I made the comment to those in attendance that we were young, slow, unproven, but besides all of that, I was optimistic because we had number 24 on our side. Joel was our one wild card and if he could stay healthy, we sincerely sensed that we would be competitive and stay close in every game, and maybe, even repeat another championship run.

Our first game of the 1993 season pitted perennially strong football programs against one another, Seton Catholic out of Binghamton and Elmira Notre Dame.

Although both teams were young, the game featured two rugged running backs cut from similar molds, Brian Cosmello of Seton, and our Joel Stephens. Close to the same size and proportions, Joel's speed and other intangibles clearly separated the combatants on that Saturday evening. Notre Dame won this road game, 35-9. Joel rushed for 190 yards on 19 carries and found the end zone twice.

Our next game was a one point loss to arch rival, Corning East. In the last minute of play, they scored on a kickoff return and a two point conversion to beat us by one. Joel never missed a game or practice because of an injury and played the last three and one half quarters with a bad turf toe that limited his cuts and drive. Never one to make excuses for a subpar performance, he just shrugged it off and looked ahead to better days. Although Joel would never voice it aloud, I knew he was not happy that the East players carried their coach off the field as if they had just won the Super Bowl.

This to him, and to many of us, was worse than celebrating on the Crusader mascot in the middle of the field at the end of a game. Redemption in his mind was put on temporary hold, but we knew that we would see them again next season, almost one year to the date of this minor blip on our radar screen. After this heartbreaker, the team rededicated themselves and proceeded to reel off five straight lopsided wins. Joel never wanted to embarrass or humiliate anyone, and during this stretch, asked to be taken out once the game was in hand. This was usually at halftime, or after the first offensive series of the third quarter. I hesitate to guess what his numbers would have been if he wasn't the class act his proud parents shaped him to be.

At this time, Joel was being noticed and actively pursued by many major colleges and universities. He was mature and savvy enough to know that eventually he would have to make a very difficult decision – football or baseball. But then again, he might pursue a two-sport college career while majoring in sports medicine. He was zeroing in on Notre Dame's rushing record held by Bob Grosvenor (Syracuse University) and was not far off the area's all-time mark held by Orlando Smith (Cincinnati University). Records and personal glory, however, were always distant in Joel's mind.

The ego and vanity of the Emperor Napoleon was vividly portrayed throughout his life as well as in his death. History has noted that he was buried down in a sunken floor of a magnificent cathedral. This was done so that everyone had to bend (bow) down to view him, and to honor him. Joel Stephens had no ego, and he did not want others to put him on display. As a reluctant celebrity, he quickly diverted any compliments and admiration to others, his main concern always being team before self. Sometimes, it almost seemed his greatest joy came from watching the success of others.

I once asked him what he saw when he was running, breaking tackles, or making razor cuts against the grain of the field. He mentioned that it seemed like the game to him was always in slow motion, making it easy for him to visualize holes and openings, or making reads or interpreting what defenders and opponents were trying to do. I guess the great ones have this as a characteristic trademark in their arsenals.

His achievements of breaking the 1,000 yard and the 2,000 yard barriers were done faster than anyone before him, and at an earlier age than anyone in Twin Tiers history. Joel commented when a reporter made him aware of this statistic that he was fortunate that he had the opportunity, and that he was proud that he could take advantage of playing behind some pretty good blockers.

I had one rule for our players when speaking to the press. If you are giving credit to others, you will never say the wrong thing. No one exemplified this rule better than Joel Stephens, but I never had to tell him either. He just knew in his heart that that was the correct thing to do. Joel felt bad about his old Williamson High School and former teammates struggling to win games in some of their sports, but he truly felt that he belonged at Notre Dame High School. His Pennsylvania friends affectionately chided him, but they were in attendance at games and supportive and rooting for him whenever the opportunity presented itself. Joel was being recruited by the likes of Syracuse, Maryland, Pitt, and Rutgers, but he still remained humble about his gifts and talents. Yes, he did possess some God-given abilities and that is what made him good. However, his work ethic, dedication, attitude, personality, and unselfishness are what made him great. Next to Ernie Davis, he was the best all-around athlete to grace the fields and courts in a little town along the Chemung River in the last 35 years.

On Friday, October 30, 1993, we faced a showdown for the divisional title versus an undefeated, high-powered, old style Wing-T group of blue collar farm boys from Whitney Point. Early miscues put us down 13-0 at the end of the first quarter. Our defensive coordinator, Dick Craft, quickly made constructive adjustments, and offensively we decided to let Joel take over the game. He lugged, twisted, churned, and turned his way for a 200-yard rushing evening, to go along with

3 touchdowns, and two interceptions in bringing us back for a 26-20 come from behind win. Lost in this emotional win for the Crusader faithful was the school rushing record bestowed on a good old plow boy from northern Pennsylvania. When asked about his achievement, Joel's only comment, made in a respectful manner, was that he didn't care to discuss it because he felt his job was to try and get us into the postseason, and do whatever it took for us to advance.

Then it was on to postseason where our next opponent was arguably the best program in the section, the Walton Warriors. This game pitted the brute strength ground-and-pound approach of Walton and its Delaware Wing T offense, against the finesse, spread-them-out balanced attack from Notre Dame. With Notre Dame down 19-14 and with less than one minute remaining in the game, Joel Stephens took a little swing pass and stepped through two defenders. With daylight ahead and no one in sight for the next 70 yards, Jason LaTourette, a 6'4" all-state linebacker dove and tripped Joel for a game saving, clutch tackle that secured a Walton win. Walton continued on their quest and won the state title, never really being challenged along the way.

What was often overlooked in recognizing Joel as a complete football player was how he played defense, reacted, read plays, pursued, and was so adept at blistering and tackling people with the ball. He was a great cover man, possessing exceptional leaping ability, many times soaring over receivers for incredibly acrobatic circus catches. He returned punts and only once in his career did he ever fumble, and he made big time amends for it. For all his efforts, he was voted a unanimous selection for all-league, all-metro, and the all-state teams, one of only three juniors in the state to fall in this elite group. He was also becoming a frequent speaker on the banquet circuit. It seemed as if once a week, Joel was being asked to tell his stories and his recipe for success at Catholic Youth Organizations, Pop Warner and Little League banquets, and for a number of other benevolent and charitable community groups. With his coach not one to pass up a free meal, as

Joel knew, I often accompanied him on his parades through various gyms and cafeterias. He was a great speaker who could captivate an audience with all eyes riveted on him as he delivered his message. He always spoke of having your priorities in the correct order, that being God, family, academics, and sports. After these gatherings, Joel usually spent another 45 minutes to an hour signing autographs and talking to people. If people were kind enough to talk to him, he certainly could find the time to return the favor. He was too young and naïve to ever notice, but I thought some of the older mothers were taken by Joel's good looks and his congeniality, and that they were coyly flirting with him.

Chapter 7

Junior Year – Basketball

Joel, beaten, stiff, sore, and bruised from a demanding and lengthy football season, willed himself to experience outstanding basketball and baseball seasons to the surprise of no one. The basketball team was undersized and with Joel as our tallest player, I placed them on what I called a two year plan to success. We had to put in the time and effort to improve our skills, and we were not going to do it overnight if we wanted to compete for championships. We played for championships and titles because they are not political; they are won and lost on the fields or courts of battle, and banners are hung in the gyms so people and players for a long time can look up and see them, and take pride in them. Joel certainly was our basketball team's leader and best player, drawing double teams and gimmick defenses in every game that were designed by opposing coaches to stop him from scoring. He was a strong rebounder and a tenacious defender. He handled the ball well with either hand, but what really astounded people was his range and accuracy shooting the ball. His jump shot was precision, with a release that was as fast as lightning, helping him to lead the team in scoring with an 18.5 average, shooting over 50% from the field. That is not too shabby for a kid who just picked up a basketball two years earlier. If he had any difficulty scoring from the field because of defenses geared to containing him or if he had an off night, Joel would simply slash and cut his way, taking the ball to the front of the rim, clenching the ball with his vice-like grip, getting fouled in the process, thus getting himself to the free throw line. At the charity stripe, Joel connected at an 82% clip, something that is phenomenal for any player at any level, and truly remarkable for a high school junior.

Teams could never completely shut him down because he could dominate with his strength and quickness at either end of the court. Even though I felt Joel played basketball only to stay in shape for football and baseball, he never loafed, relaxed, or wasted time. He always wanted to win in any game, practice, or drill in which he participated. Joel would let you know that the mental portion of sports was not a water faucet, something that you could turn on and off. He felt that people should pride themselves in doing their best, in striving to constantly do it better and more proficiently, whether playing sports or cleaning streets. And you should do it that way all the time. I have never seen anyone that lived by this doctrine more than Joel Stephens. He played hard. He played clean. He played within the rules of the game, and he always gave the utmost respect and showed class and sportsmanship to his opponents, and to their followers.

Chapter 8

Our One Disagreement

The junior baseball season brought the same successes for Joel, where once again he displayed his exceptional skill and his keen knack for knowing and understanding the game. He led the team in homeruns, steals, runs batted in, on base percentage, all the while carrying a league leading .447 batting average. From his center field position, Joel tracked down fly balls as fast as a gazelle, and with an urgency and hunger similar to a mountain lion going after its prey. He was so fluid and effortless that normally tough plays were routine putouts for this graceful individual. By this time, pro scouts were regularly inquiring about his disposition, his thoughts on a pro baseball career, and whether he would forego his college education. In addition to the pro baseball scouts, he was getting numerous solicitations and serious interest by what many would consider football factories and football programs at all levels up and down the East Coast. There were even some decent Division II schools entertaining the possibility of giving Joel a basketball scholarship after leaving high school.

During the spring baseball season, Joel had a problem with his skin. He was breaking out and getting rashes, and mentioned to me that he was tired and rundown. I knew that he had been going incessantly for 365 straight days, never letting his body recover, recuperate, and mend. His father would hear him at 3:00 and 4:00 in the morning, hitting baseballs down stairs into a net, or spot him putting his sneakers on, preparing to run the hills. He looked to be drawn and dragging, especially when it came to his Chemistry class. Maybe his batteries need to be recharged, or the medicine for his skin ailment was sapping his energy. Later on, it often crossed my mind, whether or not this skin irritation was an omen, a precursor to what was in store for him some five years later. Joel's teacher, as well as myself, felt that his effort and commitment to the course was considerably less than what was expected from him. It seemed so out of context, and uncharacteristic of everything Joel stood for that he was not doing what was required of him to successfully complete and pass the class. His teacher, Ms. Ann Koenig, an outstanding instructor, demanded an honest effort on a daily basis. She was tough, but always fair, and she was an avid supporter of Joel, just not in this particular case. Joel was dating a girl on a regular basis and this, coupled with his other interests, certainly taxed his body. He may have felt that he was just going to coast through this Chemistry class with the possibility of dropping it before taking his final exam without penalty. Neither the school, the teacher, his guidance counselor, nor his coach was going to let him off the hook He had time to get his grade up to a passing average, but he decided not to take that avenue.

This was one time when we did not see eye to eye. It temporarily strained our friendship and the strong bond that we had developed over the previous years. The school took the position that Joel would either have to buckle down and pull off this task of passing the final, or suffer the consequences and fail. I called Joel into my office and explained the situation and we had an impassioned discussion to say the least, all the while, neither one of us budging in our thinking. I realized that Joel had given a great deal of himself to his school, to me, and to countless others. I understood that he was running somewhat on empty, but I stressed to him that I had never known him to quit on something, or tackle an obstacle half-heartedly. To me, if he did that, then it would be easier for him to give that same lack of effort somewhere else down the road, possibly even in a fourth down and one with the game on the line. The bottom line was that he could be mad at me if he wished, but I was not bending on this one. I am sure that Ron and Joyce Stephens may have disagreed with this stance; at least I felt Ron and I might have been using the same book but perhaps, were not on the same page. I understood that this situation might cause the Stephens family to look at the possibility of Joel attending another school, but I felt strongly in the position that we took in dealing with this issue. It was April 1, 1993 and I told Joel he was going to hear it from me, and no one else. "If you are at Notre Dame strictly to play sports and not work in the classroom with the same intensity you show on the fields, then you are here for all the wrong reasons." Deep down my thoughts were, "How can I be so tough and hard with this person who I truly look up to as a role model for my own behavior?" To this day, I still remember WWJD. This stands for "What Would Jesus Do?" which I try to follow, but I also ask myself just as often, "What Would Joel Do?" Upon entering my house that evening, I told my wife Jayne, that we needed to say some prayers and light some candles at church because there was a possibility that Joel Stephens was going to leave Notre Dame. The first words out of my wife's mouth were, "Ha, Ha, April Fool's!" It was April Fool's Day but I was not kidding. She needed to start praying as I requested, or she was going to see a grown man begin to cry. One thing I have learned to do over the years is never to tell my wife what to do. Having been raised in a devout Christian family where there were seventeen brothers and sisters, she could handle anyone with her quick wit and her savvy in knowing how to get her next meal, swapping clothes so she never wore the same outfit twice, and making it through life anyway she could. Then too, she has always been a great believer in the power of the rosary, and I was soliciting her help. Joel was never disrespectful to anyone, and he and I would continue for a month to have small talk in the halls, and at various sporting events.

Joel loved my wife and understood that many times, she was a blessed buffer between player and coach, especially when it came to understanding my slightly, over-the-top critical thinking. My paranoia and sometimes negative thinking does get the better of me, and I was sure that the parting of Joel from Notre Dame was inevitable. Jayne is easy to talk with and she listened to Joel. She explained that I just wanted him to make good decisions, both as an athlete and as a student, and it wasn't anything personal. She did advise Joel not to make any snap judgments on his future, and that she would pray for things to get back to normal. I hoped that the scenario would play itself out in regards to the Chemistry class and end with Joel staying at Notre Dame for his senior season. Joel did bring it together and turn it on in the last few weeks of the semester, raising his failing grade to just above passing. I knew that in September, he would be going for the all time rushing record in our area and section; I just wasn't sure what school he would be doing it for. Thank God, and thanks to the prayers by Jayne, he decided to stay at Notre Dame. With an added twist, Joel was not satisfied with mediocrity and decided to attend summer school and retake Chemistry and Trigonometry to hopefully raise his borderline passing grades. He was contemplating getting involved in the game of golf and I saw him a few times over the summer on the links. It did cross my mind how good he could be at this endeavor too, if he ever decided to be serious about it. I recall one time observing him playing soccer in Mr. Weber's gym class and thinking that he was the best soccer player in the school. A number of his classmates during the scrum could not defend him, or strip him of the multi-colored ball. In the golf clubhouse, I asked him how summer school was going and he said that it was going well, and once again, he looked to be in tremendous physical condition. He then was just less than 6'2" tall and weighed 200 pounds. I asked him if he was working out and he told me he was doing some cardio running, along with some sprint work with two car tires wrapped around his waist. I mentioned to him that I was also carrying two retreads around my midsection; however, mine were permanently attached for longer than I care to imagine. With his wry and sardonic smile, he shook his head, laughed and proceeded to go to the first tee and hit a 280-yard drive, striping the first fairway. Yeah, I thought, must be beginner's luck.

It was time for summer school grades to be posted and I knew Joel was doing well in his math class. Joel's teacher was Tim Decker, a person I have known for some time. Tim was an official, a coach, and a public high school teacher, and athletic director in the area. I was comfortable enough contacting him, and I periodically checked on Joel's progress. Tim became a close friend to Joel over that summer, and he was true and loyal, right to the end. Joel had this panache and charisma that people of all ages and professions instantly migrated towards. It wasn't that big of a surprise that he had made another ally along his travels. Joel went on to ace the New York State Regents math class, and I was somewhat surprised to learn that he also received an A in Chemistry. To be honest, it wasn't just a mild surprise, but rather a huge lightning bolt from the blue that stunned me momentarily. I did not imagine that he would do that well, especially during the busy, and distracting summer months, and this one caught me completely off guard. Joel was more than capable of getting 90's in any class but in this one, I figured possibly a C, maybe even a B minus at best. I just couldn't picture in my wildest dreams, that he would get an A in his least favorite and final science class.

One of the greatest rewards on earth is to accomplish something others say is impossible. Was an A in Chemistry impossible for him? Some may have thought so but then again, this was Joel Stephens and he attacked every challenge as a personal opportunity to shine, and to prove others wrong.

Chapter 9

Senior Year Pre – Season

Joel entered the 1994 football season needing 1,161 yards to break Orlando Smith's all-time rushing record for the Elmira, Corning, and the Northern Tier of Pennsylvania regions. Even though Joel was our returning all-state running back, he had very little depth or experience to help him with the duties required for success on that year's squad. Outside of Howard Hodder, Mike Berrettini, and Matt Cornacchio helping to offset one man's responsibilities, it was not considered by many to be one of our better teams. However, they were a great bunch of guys that gave everything they had, and then some, always leaving everything out on the field. We also had our durable and muscular workhorse to give the ball to some 25 to 30 times a game, which proved to be the great equalizer.

People had come to expect Notre Dame at the very least, to win the divisional title, but that year we were not the clear cut favorites. Joel Stephens had to be the master architect if we were going to succeed, and he needed to stay healthy. A week prior to our opening night, we were scheduled to scrimmage Sayre High School from Pennsylvania, and the largest school at the time from our area, the Southside Green Hornets. The scrimmage eventually was moved from Saturday to Monday night because of inclement weather and poor playing conditions. The coaching staff knew that if we overused any of our front line players during this clash of three schools, we would be jeopardizing our chance for a win on Saturday once our regular season began. We made the decision to use Joel only sparingly in this scrimmage, while trying to

31

keep everyone else as healthy as we could. The day before, our local newspaper came out with their football tab, doing articles and over 60 pages of commentaries on all the area teams. There were two big pictures of Joel, one of which was just a headshot of him with his helmet on, eye glare in position, attentive blues fixed, and perspiration glistening on his face. This picture filled the entire front page and captured what I would from that day on refer to as "the look." This "look" illustrated Joel's persona and focus that came over him while he was preparing for every battle.

Joel's focus was evident before every game.

Walking with gear in hand towards Sayre Indian Stadium, the Southside contingent of players was arriving at the same time with competitors from both teams attempting to squeeze into the same narrow entrance. A number of the Hornet team members casually but strategically strolled by and mingled in with our players, in particular Joel Stephens, rudely making condescending and demeaning remarks. "Hey paperboy, we will see how good you really are," "You are just a big fish in a little pond," and "We will wipe that smile off your face pretty boy" were just a few that are appropriate for print. Joel, always being Mr. 120 over 80, made no comments in return. However, his easily excitable and fly-off-the-handle head coach murmured that we would use Joel as much as needed to send a statement to these cocky hooligans, and to hell with the rest of the season. Luckily, when the scrimmage started, my better judgment took over. On the first play, Joel broke two tackles at the line of scrimmage and blew past their corps of linebackers and defensive backs for a 60-yard touchdown run. The Southside defense in a state of bewilderment still wasn't sure what had just happened. On our next offensive possession, Joel took the handoff from Chris Madigan, stepped through a great cross-block from Mike Berrettini and Brad Polk, continued to run over their all-state linebacker, engraving cleat marks up the front of his jersey, and left the other defenders in his blinders en route to another 40 yards for a score.

It was gratifying to me knowing that just about every opposing player that evening came up to Joel, complimented him on his ability, and wished him the best of luck during the season. This respect, given to him from his peers, was offered without Joel uttering a single word, other than to say thanks in his soft-spoken, barely audible tone. I was pleased, almost ecstatic, knowing that "my" message to our opponents was delivered and Joel was the mailman. More importantly, Joel was healthy, rested, and his evening was completed after only two carries. Next, it was on to scheduled games where scoring more than the opposition was imperative.

Chapter 10

Opening Game Redemption

On Saturday night, September 3, 1994, the number one mission on the mind for our unpretentious, unassuming, modest superstar from Notre Dame was to erase the bad recollection from the prior year's debacle. Joel had the distinctive capacity to visualize the smallest of details, and retain the minutest information encoded in the confines of his computer-like mind. Joel vividly recalled the end of last year's game, a victory celebration by Corning's silver and burgundy as a result of their last minute winning drive. This rematch once again pitted a hard-hitting, street-tough group of well-coached players from Corning East High School against a group of baby-faced, intelligent, often pampered bunch of Catholic school choirboys. During the first quarter on a hot, humid Saturday evening, a speedy, solidly built Jake Rogers of Corning blindsided Joel, causing the ball to become dislodged from his grasp. This resulted in Joel's first, and only fumble of his career, and no one particularly cared to be in the general vicinity while he was walking off the field and coming to our sidelines. They just knew this turnover would not sit well with someone that demanded perfection from himself and who might just have cost his teammates a game. The stands were filled with an estimated 3,500 spectators. This number was insignificant if you watched football in Texas or Florida, but this figure was quite noteworthy for a high school game held in the Southern Tier of New York. Most people in attendance had the same gut wrench feeling as myself when Joel turned the ball over and that was to be ready because now all they had done was to tick him off. On Joel's next carry from scrimmage, he literally laid out 6 of the 9 defenders trying to tackle him, making them spin like props on a helicopter and putting them in a temporary la-la land. They were slow to recover, taking a few plays to clear the cobwebs from their heads and struggling to regain their composure for some more football. Father McDonough, our school's elder Jesuit priest, who is a diehard football fanatic, described this bruising, punishing run as the greatest he had ever witnessed. He was a chaplain at schools and colleges where a handful of players had careers playing in the NFL, so he was not just blowing smoke. When Father McDonough spoke, people felt the Lord himself wouldn't interrupt. Joel continued to impress – churning, twisting, pulling, grinding, and plowing his way for 261 yards on 25 carries and three touchdowns in a 24-13 win at Corning Memorial Stadium. The Crusaders outgained the Trojans by almost a four to one margin, and it probably was the most one-sided 11-point loss you would ever see. We had installed a new offense for this game, designed to get the ball to Joel with the idea of either misdirecting opponents by using decoys, fakes and counters, or providing Joel with as many blockers in front of him that was legally possible.

The players executed the game plan to perfection and once again, we had people beginning to think we were the team to beat. On the defensive side of the ball, Joel had a notable game as well. In the waning moments of the fourth quarter, he recovered a fumble and returned it for a touchdown. This play secured our opening day victory and laid the foundation for future successes. Randy Holden, the gruff and intense Corning East coach, stated after the game that "Joel Stephens didn't beat us, but rather he bludgeoned us to death. He truly is the real deal!" Walking off the field to the locker room, I noticed some of the players who had made comments at the scrimmage the previous week standing in the lobby outside the team dressing room. Chiding them I posed the question, "Is he still just a big fish in a little pond?" The all-state linebacker who may still be sporting Joel's cleat marks on his V-shaped chest politely responded, "Coach, he would be the kingfish in any body of water as far as I'm concerned." It avenged a 15-14 upset loss to Corning the previous year, and it lifted a huge weight that helped to clear our team's psyche, putting everyone in a good space for the remainder of that season. It also set the tone for a bitter and rancorous rivalry with Corning East for the next ten years.

Chapter 11

Home Opener

As the train rumbled down the tracks behind our school's football stadium early in the third quarter during our first home game, one couldn't help but think of the Notre Dame offense, especially Joel Stephens. Joel scored five touchdowns in his first five possessions as the Crusaders pounded fellow Catholic school rival, Binghamton Seton High. The final damage for Joel in this 41 – 24 victory was 27 carries for 246 yards, five touchdowns, and a reception for 18 yards. These individual totals were done, surprisingly, in two and one half quarters. We gained 451 yards in all, and quite honestly, could have gained more. Dave Johnson, the head mentor for the opposition, stated, "We were totally prepared for this game, and prepared for ten players. You just can't prepare for that eleventh and the destruction that Joel Stephens can inflict. He is too strong, too tough to knock off his feet, and he is such a tremendous athlete; he is just an outstanding young man." Touchdowns by the Saints late in the third quarter and early in the fourth made this seem like a close blowout. I wanted Joel to impress in every game, which I was confident he would do. The reality was that neither Joel nor myself ever wanted to humiliate another team or program. The tributes, accolades, and soon-to-be-broken records were warranted, but they were something that Joel never thought about, or was comfortable with. Joel could care less about his name in any record book, but his teammates and coaches really wanted it for him. Joel continually was the talk of the fans in the stands during every game. People would turn to one another and ask, "How many yards does he have now?" These 200 plus rushing yard totals have become more common in the last several years; however, they were remarkable, stirring, and more noteworthy back in 1994. Former University of Notre Dame Coach Lou Holtz once commented that the Fighting Irish fans of South Bend did not want to worry about winning a game after halftime. Thanks to the running of Joel Stephens, first half fumble recoveries by Tim O'Herron, Peter Duchy, and Howard Hodder, and an offense that was hitting on all cylinders, our players put us in a comfortable 26-0 halftime lead. After the game and in typical Joel Stephen's fashion, he praised his offensive line, stating that they were simply awesome. They did do well, but it was also the second, third, and extra efforts by our star that accounted for his totals.

Joel's ability and athleticism was constantly on display.

Barry Svrugla, sports writer for the *Corning Leader,* had just arrived in our area from his home in New England. His first assignment was to attend the game at Notre Dame and see what all the fuss was about concerning the running back who had dissected Corning's team a week earlier. What he saw was a man playing against boys, a monster truck battling go-carts in a demolition derby. He saw someone who would run over, through, around, and past hapless defenders. He saw him find a small crease in the line of scrimmage and turn it into a mini highlight reel. He saw him get hit in the backfield by a host of defensive players and still gain positive yardage. He witnessed Joel beating a defensive back to the corner where he turned and made a lunging one-hand catch. One game is not enough to make a complete evaluation of a player, at least not typically. As Barry later wrote in the *Corning Leader*, "When I arrived at Notre Dame on this evening, I fully expected to be disappointed." Having watched a number of major college football games, he thought Joel would be just another run of the mill, small town hero, never making it beyond the village pub, reminiscing the old days five years in the future. He thought that there was no way this high school hotshot could duplicate his output from the Corning East game. Here, Barry finally got one right. He didn't duplicate that feat; Joel one-upped his effort. Barry wrote that, "It reminded [him] of the old days when black and white television was in vogue, and when strong, young men played a smash-mouth style of football in front of enthusiastic crowds that whispered their names back and forth, wondering what college would be lucky enough to get them." Joel was this throwback to the old days when players were genuine on the field and even more genuine when they were out of their element, and of course, out from under the spotlight. A time or two while we were alone, I commented to Joel that some of the things he did were awesome but his standard response to me was, "Coach, how many times do I have to tell you? I'm not awesome, but rather the

Lord is, and he is in everyone one of us." Yeah Joel, OK, whatever you say, but that was Joel: true, authentic, and "awesome"!

Joel was heavily pursued to sign either a Division I, full ride football and / or baseball scholarship. A true star's college choice is anticipated as much as his next homerun or touchdown run. Joel used some of the same, slippery moves in his arsenal that he used on the football field to dodge this question when strangers asked what sport he would prefer to take to the next level. I think these autograph seekers left with the impression that he wanted to play both. Joel was faced with a doubly tough decision to sign early. He could play baseball at Clemson, the number one ranked baseball school in the country, or go somewhere else and play football. Just as any normal kid, Joel truly wanted the chance to thoroughly enjoy his senior year, playing his heart out in both sports, sandwiched around his all star basketball career. After taking an official football visit to Syracuse, he was discussed in every recruiting magazine across the U.S., and solicited to join the likes of Maryland, North Carolina State, Penn State, Clemson, and Syracuse, a university that had already spiced the deal by making an offer of a full scholarship. The Southern Tier College Prospect Group headed by Ed Dean and which covers a 90 plus school area, had made Joel their top attraction. Many of the colleges projected him as a defensive back, or as a strong safety because of his speed, size, and ability to put some pretty good hits on people. College defensive coaches also liked his anticipation and reaction to schemes and sets run by other teams. As a strong safety, Joel thought that every pass thrown by an opposing quarterback had the stamp, "Property of Joel Stephens," engrained on it. Syracuse was a bit different in that he was one of their top five recruits, but the position coaches had been feuding about who would be acquiring his services. Each coach wanted him to play at his own area of coaching expertise - fullback, defensive back, strong safety, flanker, or maybe even a receiver. If they felt he could play any of these positions, I guess it wasn't a misnomer when people said he was "an athlete."

Two weeks after Labor Day, the weather was torrid as a new school week began. Throughout the week, a number of players remained nicked and bruised from the prior two contests. Regardless, everyone was ready for the game on Saturday night. The Friday before the game, a welcome frosh dance had been scheduled by the student council. It is always a coach's fear that either the team will lose its focus, or somebody is going to get hurt in the "mosh pit" on the dance floor. My wife suggested that I might be getting too old for chaperoning these events, many times coming home upset with the shenanigans of a few players.

After Friday's shorter practice, we made our way to the chapel for the team Mass. The night before every game, the players and coaches crowded into a little chapel, and attended liturgy led by Father McDonough. We went to this vigil right from practice without showering and to say the smell was ripe on a number of occasions would be an understatement. If God and Father didn't mind, I guess my prominent Italian nose could live with it for forty-five minutes as well. There were always a few Sisters of Mercy who joined us as we prayed for various intentions – our health, our families, passing exams, and of course, winning the football game. At most of these services, a little revered eighty-something-year-old nun named Sr. Berchmans Ross joined the team. She was 4'8" with silver white hair, gleaming eyes and a love that could fill ten gymnasiums. We had some players, in particular Ari Salsburg, a 300 lb. weightlifter who could crush an extremity when shaking hands during the offering of peace. With Sister's frail hands anxious to greet any takers, Joel would jump in between Sister and Ari because our lineman didn't know his own strength at times. We didn't need any injuries, especially one that occurred at Mass. Joel and Sister absolutely loved each other, and were best of friends. He always made it a point to treat her extra special and give her a big hug during this weekly ritual. I can honestly say that I had never seen Joel upset. However, I would venture to say that if any student was uninformed or misinformed about Joel's concern for Sister, and they caused any type of disturbance or misbehaved in her class, Joel might have had a little attitude adjustment for that particular individual.

Father McDonough gave the homily and somehow, he tied in Christ, football, life, and how it played into everyone's continued existence, journey, and final destination. Father attentively listened to me whine all week long about the seemingly insurmountable obstacles we faced in our upcoming game. Jesuits are known for their intelligence and rational thinking. Many felt that if the school ever needed to get out of debt, we should submit Father's name to become a contestant on "Jeopardy" or "Who Wants To Be A Millionaire." A man who can speak seven different languages, has a double doctorate, and loves football can't be that bad. As intelligent as he is, he explained the gospel in layman's terms, what was expected from us in relationship to our beliefs, and how we should conduct ourselves in victory or defeat. Every player's eyes were riveted on Father when he spoke, but Joel seemed to be almost trance-like, focusing on every word throughout the Mass. Father chose the passages for each Mass and Joel did the readings.

Whether sharing opinions or fears, or dealing with problems confronting us in our daily lives, Father McDonough has been the one constant that has always been there for our football program. The players and coaches always appreciated his faithful support throughout the decades. Joel knew how uncomfortable it was to ride a team bus on a long trip, especially for someone up in years like Fr. McDonough. He mentioned to me that he valued Father McDonough even more for never missing one of our trips, no matter what distance we had to travel.

Next up for the Crusaders was a recently struggling program out of Newark Valley. On film, they didn't look very talented, but they did have some decent people that could cause a dilemma. Ralph Novi's squad packed the line with nine defenders and dared Joel to find a crease. The Cardinals played hard for four quarters before finally succumbing to 90-degree heat and the Notre Dame juggernaut. Joel turned in his third straight 200 plus yards rushing game in a 35-8 divisional win.

Ian Lampman became the answer to the trivia question – Who was the blocking back for Joel Stephens in his record-breaking season? Ian studied many films of Joel and learned to develop some of the same characteristics of his senior teammate. During Ian's senior season, he rushed for over 1,000 yards, and was recruited by many Division II and Division III schools. He impressed college coaches with his cutback running ability, something that Joel worked on daily with him. Many coaches referred to him as "The Cutback Kid."

At the conclusion of the game, I was approached by Tom Hughes. Prior to the start of our season, I had been introduced to him at school. Tom had worked at *Scholastic Coach Magazine*, which is considered the bible for high school and college coaches in the country. Bruce Weber, the publisher of *Scholastic Coach Magazine*, along with Tom's help, created an awards program for high school sports and individual athletes called "The Gatorade Circle of Champions." These two men, along with Chris Lawlor, who would later become a writer for the *USA Today* in charge of their high school sports section, and Abby West, a legendary coach and athletic director from the state of New Jersey, developed the criteria used in considering each state's recipient. These winners were then measured against other states' finest, for regional and national exposure. All were very good at analyzing and evaluating the abilities of possible candidates. This program has dramatically taken off from its inception in the early 1980s with many professional superstars receiving this honor. Past winners include Peyton Manning, Emmitt Smith, Ron Powlus, and Jeff George. Tom often visited practices and games, making the trek north from his New Jersey home. He loved Joel as a player, and he had even higher regard for him as a person. At the time, our football program used his marketing services, not knowing that he was involved in the Gatorade program. Down the road and thanks to Tom, we would learn that Joel had earned one of the game's highest honors for a high school player.

Next it was on to Corning West, a team coached by one of my favorite former players, Mike Johnston Jr. Mike's dad is a legendary football and basketball coach in the Southern Tier. It was under Mike Sr.'s tutelage that members of the Notre Dame staff developed many of our ideas about coaching, training and conditioning. He was also one of Joel's biggest fans. Going up against young Mike and with his father giving advice from the press box, it was very similar to playing our own team. On this evening, we faced an abundance of matching plays, comparable formations, as well as assorted defensive alignments that were difficult to separate. Motivated by the fact that the Johnstons were Notre Dame alumni, they would assuredly have their players ready to play inspired ball for the full forty-eight minutes. Early on, the game took on the appearance of a heavyweight boxing contest

It was a dreary, rainy night on our home field when two friends opposed each other for the first and only time. Mike Jeronimo, Joel's freshmen year buddy who transferred, was the fullback and main weapon for Corning West. Mike toughed it out and had a decent game, rushing for 100 yards on 27 carries. Joel had the edge with 22 carries for 186 yards and two scores. Someone said to me walking off the field that Jeronimo really came to play. I nodded my approval and replied, "But Stephens came to win!" Joel and the offensive line scored a pair of second quarter knockdowns, and held on for a 13-0 win over a very stubborn Corning West group.

Later that evening, Joel let someone borrow his car so he walked two miles back to my house. He wanted to call his dad for a ride, but I volunteered to give him a lift home. At 11:00 p.m. on a dark road with cow fields on both sides, Joel noticed an elderly motorist who was stranded with a flat tire. Joel motioned for me to pull over to see if we could offer any assistance. "Please, Joel, don't make us do this" was my initial plea. Joel assured me that he could change the tire; I just needed to stay out of his way and be his lookout for oncoming cars that could get dangerously close. The owner of the car attempted to hand Joel ten dollars, but he refused to accept it. Joel just wanted to get to his bed, let his body recuperate, and begin his weekly routine once again.

Chapter 12

Game and Season Rushing Records

Trumansburg now visited "The House of Pain" also known as "The Holy Land" and Joel needed 394 yards to become the Twin Tiers all-time rushing leader. The Blue Raiders were well-coached, disciplined, and athletic. It did not matter to Joel, as he ran through their defense with the same ease that had him heading towards the top of the rushing charts. Joel eclipsed another record on that night, setting the single game rushing total with 352 yards on 25 carries. Scoring three touchdowns en route to this performance, Joel now had amassed 3,953 yards and was just 42 yards shy of the record.

Trumansburg's Coach Jack Reed commented to me at halftime, "Oh my God, he just keeps getting better." By halftime, Joel had burned Reed's defense for 240 yards and three touchdowns. He had one last carry at the end of the third quarter, bursting through a hole on the left side for 56 yards, and securing a 33-0 win, setting up a showdown with Tioga.

Joel was modest and characteristically subdued in his response to the single game rushing record. He gave praise to his offensive line, his coaching staff, Bob Grosvenor and John Maio (two stars from the past), to the vendors in the stands, announcers, half of the state of New York, and anyone else who he felt supported him on his quest.

The interviews were becoming so frequent that I could see him slip into a different state of mind – one that allowed him to stiff-arm and dodge compliments like would-be tacklers. He permitted discussion of team goals only, his interest in individual achievements falling by

46

the wayside so teammates were not alienated. This was the way Joel presented himself as more attention was paid to him. It was Joel Stephens' media mode. Behind this mode, I hoped he understood that he was pretty special. In five games, he had rumbled his way for 1,202 yards. That alone would be a reason to boast and become aloof. He often reminded me, "It is more important to be a good person than it is to be a star."

Speaking to reporters, Joel never cracked or wavered one iota. He talked about his linemen. During a practice, a television cameraman asked what the breaking of the Section IV rushing record would mean to him. "It would be great for Notre Dame," Joel replied simply. The reporter kept the pressure on about eclipsing records. "Records are good, but I would trade any record for a state title any day." Whoever said that there is no interest like self-interest never met Joel Stephens. I can verify that this humility and candor was not an act. Joel's philosophy was to give credit to others so that you would never say the wrong thing. This affectionately labeled country bumpkin sincerely believed that he was where he was because of his 30 other teammates. "He is just his normal self all the time," said junior quarterback, Chris Madigan. "He is so modest. He doesn't brag at all." This modesty was even prevalent at the Stephens' home. "Joel has pretty much excelled in everything he has done," said his father, Ron Stephens. But around the household, Joel was not granted any special perks. He had his chores and duties, and the treatment was the same for all the Stephens' kids.

Much of Joel's successes, foremost the 3,953 yards that left him 525 yards short of the Section IV all-time record set by Hancock's Elbert Allen, was a direct result of his physical attributes. Joel, quite simply, was constructed like a football player. Here was a rock solid 6'2", 205-pound specimen that struck fear in the hearts of players on the opposing side of the ball by his mere presence. Joel was so strong, so powerful, so well built; he never went down with first contact. Nobody put him down on one hit. Nobody. Joel was not simply a power back, but rather he was just as likely to sidestep a defender, as he was to bowl one over. He ran with a purpose and he ran with the mindset that he had a point to prove. What made him even more dangerous was his vision and his ability to read and setup his blocks. Many college programs wanted him as a runner, but just as many wanted him as a strong safety on the defensive side of the ball. He knew that offense sold tickets, but defense won championships. Playing defense at the collegiate level would be just fine with Joel; he did like to hit people full boar on the football field which was contrary to his gentleness off the field. Ball carriers and receivers were constantly aware of his whereabouts. Most of all, he liked playing good defense because he knew that it brought team recognition.

A bittersweet experience was in store for us upon our visit to Tioga Central. Tioga was coached by one of the all time win leaders in New York State. Coach Jim Haggerty started at Elmira Notre Dame in the 1950s, and he continued to coach at the high school until 2005. He has more than 250 victories to his credit and many championships as well. This game was supposed to be a celebration, a victory, and a record-breaking gala for Joel Stephens and the Notre Dame Crusaders.

Someone forgot to tell the proud unit from Tioga. Notre Dame could not do anything right on that day, and the Tigers capitalized at every opportunity, blasting their way to a 52-14 win. This was the worst and most lopsided loss we had in my fourteen years at the helm. Jason Bellis, the Tioga quarterback ran the triple option to perfection, concealing the ball and selling his fakes like a stage magician in a football uniform. He hid the ball from everyone and our defense had no clue as to its whereabouts. We also felt our defensive aggressiveness was a disadvantage against this offense. Joel did set the record on that day, but he felt that he had let everyone down, especially his grandparents, Emmett and Virginia Stephens, and Arthur and Marjorie Swanson, who were at the game.

He got a bad hip-pointer late in the first quarter that seriously affected his play during the rest of the game. Give Joel the chance to make and excuse and you would still be waiting. Making alibis was one game he didn't play. It was apparent early on that he was not himself, but Joel gave credit where credit was due. "Tioga was the better prepared team on this Saturday." He also admitted that this was the most demoralizing loss he had ever had to deal with. Joel's record was a happy footnote to a very sad and depressing day. I went home that evening and lay on the couch through the night, not once getting up to eat, or answer the phone. At 10:30 p.m., we heard a knock at our front door and our unexpected visitor was carrying a large cheese pizza. It was Joel, wanting to make sure that I was OK. He figured that if I would eat, eventually I would return to normal. He was in some pain, but did not care to discuss it. His steadfast approach to life was to reach out and help others anyway humanly possible. We discussed the game very little, watched some football on television, and chatted about what was in store for Sunday morning. According to my wife and Joel, it was not an option to miss Sunday Mass simply because I didn't want to explain the loss, or rehash the particulars with anyone. They made me realize that people really didn't give a cat's meow about Notre Dame football, and that attending Mass is an obligation. We arrived barely on time for the 11:00 a.m. service at St. Casmir's Church and while receiving the Eucharist, an unfamiliar priest said, "Body of Christ, sorry about the loss yesterday, Coach, and I hope Joel is OK" as he placed the host in my open mouth. When we returned to the pew, Jayne, while shaking her head in amazement, leaned over and said, "I guess everyone does follow Joel Stephens and Notre Dame football."

Chapter 13

Crusaders Regroup

The team and the coaches were devastated by the loss, and also with the thought we could not control our own destiny in regards to the playoffs. The players bounced back about mid-week thanks to Joel and his positive response to the game. He took the burden on his shoulders for the loss, never making an excuse for his performance. I tried to give Joel an avenue out for his minimal number of carries (13 for 76 yards) referring to his debilitating hip injury but he would not buy into it. Joel knew all too well that excuses are for weak people and he would not make one. He told me that he was fine and to give him the ball. He did not miss a practice, even though we tried to keep him out. He wanted to carry the ball as many times as I would give it to him come Friday night vs. Troy High School. Joel never was one to look back, but rather he was that visionary who always looked forward to a great tomorrow. He made you feel that even if you had fallen down, at least you were still moving forward. Friday evening came, and we were all looking for redemption. Joel had unfairly shouldered the blame for the previous week, but Fr. McDonough stressed that the quality of football he loved the most is that it is truly a team sport, everyone sharing equally in both the wins and the losses. Life is full of challenges and it is how one responds to adversity that truly makes us who we are. Hardships do not build character, but rather reveal it, and we were going to see what we were made of, and how we would respond to our misfortune and the likelihood of no postseason play. Fr. McDonough lightened the atmosphere in my office two hours before kickoff by jokingly mentioning to our special teams coach, John Mirando, "I take football very seriously, almost as seriously as Lent." We all knew what

Father was really saying and that was to go out and play hard, play smart, and have fun.

Things returned to normal after our stunning loss to the Tioga Tigers. The game versus Troy from Pennsylvania was a complete rout with the outcome decided well in advance of the halftime festivities. Joel once again showed his true talent, even though fans in attendance had no idea he was still hurting from the prior week. More stinging to him than his hip was that no matter how much he gave from here on out, chances were very good that we would not have the opportunity to make postseason play. I made the decision to play Joel only on offense. Honoring his request to carry the load, he responded with a 26 carry, 251 yard, two touchdown performance, with no carries in the second half. I can be stubborn at times, but I also know who brings the dinner. The "Horse" did the work and we would sink or swim with Joel at the helm. Joel always expected a great deal from himself. He was relentless and determined not to have an emotional letdown going into that game. He was an eighteen-year-old who had almost a spiritual impact on everyone who crossed his path. Joel just didn't advocate it; he lived it in everything he did. This was a statement game and I felt that the character and integrity of our team and that of Joel Stephens certainly returned to normal. Job completed: Notre Dame 40, Troy 8.

Now it was time to prepare for the big, talented group from Moravia, a school located not too far from Syracuse. Moravia was also the team that beat Tioga, the squad that had dismantled us a few weeks prior. We all felt good, knowing that Joel was getting close to being 100%, and that they would have to make the long trek to our stadium. Some players thrive on pressure while others get unglued and come apart. I can never recall that happening with Joel. If we could win the next two games, we would at least share the divisional title, but our chances of going to a bowl game were bleak. Notre Dame squared off against a Moravia team that had a couple of Division I players on the line as well as depth, speed, and the skilled running of Jamie Randolf. We had to be very careful of not looking too far ahead to an anticipated showdown with the Walton Warriors, the # 2 team in the state. It was crucial for us to end the season with a pair of wins. Everyone was dedicated to this mission, and to help Joel earn the most prestigious football record in our section as the all time rushing leader. First and foremost was to do whatever it took to take down Moravia, and all in the know understood that the brunt of this fell squarely on the shoulders of our leader, Joel Stephens. This was the last time our seniors would grace the field at Brewer Memorial Stadium, and we always try to send them off on a memorable note. It was also the final time Number 24 thrilled the capacity home crowds with electrifying runs and graceful and acrobatic moves of strength and power that had not been seen since the days of the Elmira Express, Ernie Davis. I left one final message on the chalkboard and that was, "Keep the fire for four quarters." As we leave the locker room, it is our tradition to reach up and touch a small rectangular, soiled, and ragged old sign that simply states, "N.D. Pride." That pride and tradition, and the legs of Joel were the catalyst for our success on that beautiful, fall evening. Facing a must-win situation, our boys came through with big plays on both sides of the ball when we needed them, holding on to win a hard fought 30-21 battle. Joel wanted redemption and he got it with this win. He also got the Section IV rushing title with his 27 carry, 222 yard, 4-touchdown performance. He would have easily relinquished his individual titles and records, and all the media attention in a heartbeat if he could have replayed that Tioga game that would have kept our season perfect. However, as Joel often said, "It is what it is." Joel was now the new number one. The run that put him over the top was a typical Joel Stephens highlight reel. Early in the fourth quarter and with the score 24-21 and the outcome still in doubt, Joel took a handoff on a fourth and 6 from Moravia's 43 yard line. He broke the tackles of two defenders in our backfield, cut behind another rusher, ran back against the grain and squared his shoulders, churning and bulldozing down the left sideline. Five yards down the field, he spun off another tackler, and then dragged two more players for a 10-yard gain and a first down. With 7:56 left in the game, Joel now had achieved another record. He had amassed 1,743 yards for the season, just 179 yards short of the Twin Tiers record of 1,922 yards held by Chris Jennings from Towanda High School, set in 1987. As effortless as our star made it look, I knew eventually it wouldn't be so easy when he would have to grapple with the difficult decision to play football or baseball in less than a year from now. Barring any major injury, he would play D-1 football, D-1 baseball, or become a high draft choice by some major league baseball team.

Chapter 14

Joel's Last Football Game

As a power-hitting centerfielder, he had already impressed a number of professional baseball scouts. Many major league teams were willing to draft him at the spring meeting. He was not your average high school athlete and we were meticulously trying to make his senior year as normal, fun-filled and low-stress as possible. Even though his body was battered and bruised, we felt we succeeded in reaching our goal. We all felt sadness going into his final varsity football game. One of the great joys of being a high school coach / teacher is watching your players grow up and mature. Conversely, one of the toughest aspects of being a coach / teacher is watching your players leave the nest. This was a difficult period knowing that after that week, Joel's football career at Notre Dame would come to a conclusion, and that he no longer would be at our practices and games. Also, there was a strong possibility that he would never don a football uniform again.

Joel had been the consummate player and student of the game. Granted, he was gifted naturally, but he had continuously worked very hard to raise himself from a good athlete to a very talented one. That is what separates the great ones from the rest. He was the complete package, excelling in every phase of every sport in which he was a participant. He was so very diligent in studying his game films, and especially those of his opponents. He could break down a film, and he knew the opposition just as well as any coach on our staff. He was incredibly prepared every time he took the field. Rewards came to Joel because he had good habits. No matter what setting, he continuously pushed himself to attain a higher level of performance. His decision to play pro baseball, or opt to go to college for football and baseball had to be his, and his alone. The one constant was that he did have a great support system with his family fully behind him. He often discussed his options with his mom and dad, and sometimes with me. We were aware of what pressure and speculation could do to young men faced with similar decisions. We had heard of the horror stories of guys like Joel Stephens sent into a tailspin of depression, drugs, alcohol, and other vices. His only addiction was the need to help others. Joel was so versatile, so determined, so focused that whatever he chose, he was going to be successful and a winner. Deep down, he was content because he truly believed that Christ would provide him with guidance in coming to his final choice. When he turned his thoughts towards his religion, Joel felt that the Lord had blessed him so much. He would be as faithful and as serving to Him, as his Lord was to Joel. As needed, Joel would pray to make the correct decision, and to continue to honor the goodness of the Lord. Joel reminded me that God said in Romans 8:28, "All things work together for good."

Joel was that unique athlete who came along once every generation, if that. He had ice in his veins at the most nerve-racking times, but I think he internalized a great deal, and struggled with his notoriety. Very seldom did Joel burden others with things that were on his mind. That was how he wanted it, and I think it got old for him when people asked how he was feeling. He felt that the Lord would provide and take him under His wing, providing solace and comfort every time Joel would request to be placed in His hands. For someone who was so talented, Joel yearned for the ordinary. Here was a young man who because of his character and personality didn't create a lot of I-need-to-be-treated-special, or I-am-better-than-you, or above-you attitudes. The way he viewed things was that what he did was as important, but no more important than what others did, or gave to the team. He didn't just care about sports; he cared about everything and everybody.

Where Joel was concerned, it was always others before self. In some instances, people who face tragedy or a traumatic experience suddenly find God and become a better person. In Joel's case, he was that good person long before he ever was stricken with terminal colon cancer. It was inexplicable to Joel that one of our country's cornerstones was built on freedom of religion, but ironically, public schools could not teach religion. He enjoyed going to team Masses. He took pleasure in going to school liturgies and prayer services in which he actively participated. He could quote Bible verses in his theology classes. He treasured beginning and ending our practices and games with a prayer, something as a private Catholic school we are allowed to do. Joel's number one priority was his belief in a higher power. In his Grammy Award winning song, "Where Were You When The World Stopped Turning?" the popular Country and Western singer, Alan Jackson says the Lord gave us three things – faith, hope, and love, and the greatest is love. Joel loved the Lord, he loved people, he loved sports, and he loved life.

Getting back to Joel's last game, we needed to finish with a victory to earn a share of a divisional title, and it was important that these players be recognized for their efforts. Mid week, a close friend of mine was informed that his dad had collapsed on the golf course and never recovered. The funeral services were held on Friday and Jayne and myself paid our respects. I had not consumed alcohol for over six years, but on that Friday evening, I decide to indulge and have a few mixed drinks with grieving family members. At 10:00 p.m., I got a call from the assistant coaches that a party was in progress, and that a number of football players were in attendance. I had the coaches pick me up and take me to that party. Somewhat bold normally, and now having some added liquid courage in my system, I put the kibosh on the party and made everyone go home. The parents were home, and nothing illegal was happening, but the entire staff felt that the players needed to be rested, alert, and primed for the next day's showdown, especially with a two-hour bus ride to the game. Joel told some of his teammates that he would try to speak to me, and smooth things over. He said they were just playing cards and that the party was breaking up anyway. I cut him no slack and continued on my tirade. I overheard one of our linemen off in the distance say to Joel, "I could have smoothed it over better than that." To be honest, I have never seen thirty high school kids scatter so fast, and if they moved that quickly in fifteen hours, the Eagles of Whitney Point were going to have their hands full. The next morning, I considered my behavior of the previous evening and I called the parents who had hosted the party, John and Rita Polk, and apologized for my actions. Their son, Brad, was an all-state linebacker and one of Joel's closest friends. Less than a year after Joel succumbed to cancer, Brad was tragically murdered in Orlando, Florida, and once again, the Notre Dame faithful would have occasion to grieve.

We came out flat, and somewhat uninspired for the first half of this contest, and all I could think was, "I told you so because of the night before," but I kept that to myself. In the third quarter, we shifted into gear and after a Whitney Point turnover, Joel had a crowd-pleasing, vintage, twisting, knifing, and tackle breaking, 46-yard run to inside the ten-yard line. Bob Michaels of Elmira's WELM radio station was broadcasting the game. Bob had a special friendship with Joel. This union came from the many interviews he had done with Joel throughout his high school career as well as when he was ill. He described Joel's last run in his Notre Dame career this way: "Second and six from the ND 38. A handoff to Stephens off the right tackle. Stephens darts into the hole, sidesteps one tackler, runs over another, bursts into the clear, one defender left to beat. Stephens out runs him. He's in the clear. He's going to go all the way! Wait! He steps out of bounds on the Whitney Point five-yard line! What a classy kid!" The score at the time was Notre Dame 25, Whitney Point 0. It didn't matter that he could add one more touchdown to his already impressive resume. I never had to tell Joel. He always knew what was the proper thing to do. He never wavered and always held true to form, even when faced with split second decisions. Joel finished his fabulous career with a resounding, 23 carry, 210 yard, 3 touchdown performance, playing three quarters of the game. He also threw a 72 yard, in stride, laser strike to Mike Berrettini to break a scoreless tie in the second quarter.

We had planned all year to leave the field at the end of this regular season game as the divisional champs, regroup, get healthy, and then make a run towards sectional, regional, and state titles. We had won the divisional title, but it was a hollow celebration. Not too many teams can go 8-1 and not go on and play in some postseason game. As empty as this statement may sound, we still were champions and I felt that we were one of the best four teams in the state.

Sadly, after the interviews were done, we went back to the school to clean the locker rooms and pack our equipment for winter reconditioning. No longer would the musty, sweat drenched pads, or helmets with the etched in scratches from the opponents headgear be draping the lockers of individual players.

After the game, there were numerous press personnel huddling around the outside of our locker room, asking if Joel was available to comment on his last game, his records, and his career. I told them that he hadn't returned from the field just yet. I also suggested that if they looked for a little boy in a wheelchair, or a young girl on crutches, or any youngster that may have an injury or a disability, then they would find Joel Stephens. I added that they should please tell him that we were running out of game balls and that I would appreciate it if he could return at least the last one so that the school could have it as a keepsake. I constantly had to remind him that we were Notre Dame of Maple Avenue, not the one in South Bend with an unlimited budget, and for every game ball he gave away, I would have to purchase another one out of my own pocket to take its place. It was always a running joke between player and mentor, and I enjoyed razzing him just a bit. Reporters found Joel talking and laughing with a ten-year-old in a wheelchair, suffering with the later stages of multiple sclerosis. The boy's pain and the much lesser pain that Joel may have been experiencing as a result of possibly never playing in an official football game again, were non-existent when you looked at the pair, even from a distance. Their eyes were bright, their smiles glorious, bathing in a friendship that had developed and evolved over the past eight weeks. I always felt that after Joel's professional career, he would have made such an outstanding elementary school teacher, just like his mom. He loved kids, and he loved to make lasting memories on impressionable minds. Joel was so unique in his ability to connect with all types of people, especially the ones who may have had a handicap or a disability. As sick as this ten-year-old boy was, and as much pain as he had endured, who would have ever imagined that Joel, not long in the future, would meet a similar fate? Even though Joel realized that he had been truly blessed in so many ways, he would have instantly changed places with this youngster.

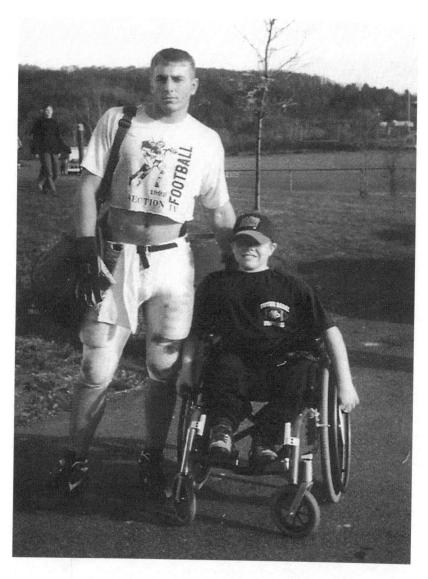

Joel sharing time with an admirer after a football game.

Joel was an enigma. He was so tough, yet he had a surreal, almost bizarre softness about him through which he opened the door to his inner feelings. He gave others a contagious joy as well as hope, in spite of odds that may have seemed insurmountable. He posed for pictures with fans and admirers, regardless of how much time it took. This caring and giving to others was demonstrated time and time again throughout the next, and his last, four years.

Joel was a regular at the "Read Aloud" programs in the grammar schools of Pennsylvania. He served as a "Big Brother" for other young boys, taking them to practices, for snacks, hunting on the farm, and everything else an older brother does for his sibling. Winning was very important to Joel, but it wasn't the most important thing. Wins and losses were just temporary. What meant the most to Joel were the friendships and close-knit bonds that he developed over the years. He had passion, he had emotion, but one of his greatest assets was his inner peace. He excelled on the fields, but he truly shined in life.

Joel finished his career with 4,715 total rushing yards, 1,954 rushing yards for the season, and with them, area and sectional records. Did Joel look to others for affirmation? No, all he wanted was to be a good teammate, and contribute in any way that he could. Joel commented that this was not a Joel Stephens record, but rather a Notre Dame team record. Instead of a swollen head, what he had was swollen muscles, with his work ethic never taking a vacation.

Joel Stephens and close friend, Brad Polk, volunteering in the " Read Aloud Program" at a Pennsylvania grammar school.

Chapter 15

Football Awards and Honors

Tom Hughes from *Coach Magazine* and the representative from the "Gatorade Circle of Champions Player of the Year" walked up to me as I was leaving the field one day. He informed me that Joel was the best high school football player he had seen through his travels throughout New York, New Jersey, and Pennsylvania, and that he was submitting his name for the New York State Player of the Year. In fact, Tom, who had been analyzing players for years, said that Joel was the best high school running back he had ever seen play. His list included such players as Willie Wilson (Kansas City Royals), Butch Woolfolk (Michigan, New York Giants), Tony Stewart (Iowa, Seattle Seahawks), Craig "Ironhead" Heyward (Pittsburgh, New Orleans Saints), and Mike Rozier (Nebraska, Heisman Trophy Winner, Houston Oilers). Besides being such a great player, Tom was quick to point out that he was such a remarkable young man, so easy to talk to, and so humble that God had blessed him.

Our season was done and all we could do was sit and wonder, "What if"?

As Willie Mays once said, "Would've, should've, could've, if, and, and but are all terms for losers." Bottom line: we did not get it done. Walton eventually won the state title, which made us feel even more miserable and depressed. Scot Taylor, a young assistant coach at Tioga, commented in the paper that a running back from Walton was the best running back in Section IV. A close friend of Scot, Terry Dougherty, a former tight end from Syracuse University, was teaching history at

Notre Dame at the time. I asked Dougherty to get the word back to Mr. Taylor that I was not happy with his comment. Two weeks later, all-star and all-state teams were published and Joel's name was at the forefront of every one. He was named the Elmira *Star-Gazette* Player of the Year, the *Corning Leader* Player of the Year, and as the First Team All-State Running Back for 1994. He also was named the New York State Player of the Year. During the next week, Joel was honored as the "New York State Circle of Champions Gatorade Player of the Year." This award has gained a reputation as an accurate measure of high school character and talent. As a state winner, Joel qualified for consideration as one of eight regional winners in the country. A $500 donation was made to our state high school's athletic association in Joel's name. The Quaker Oats Company, maker of Gatorade, sent two beautiful trophies, and two plaques. One set was for the school to keep in the auditorium display case, and the other was awarded to Joel at a school assembly. As for Scot Taylor's comment on the best running back, I offered my opinion to the Elmira *Star-Gazette* by stating, "To anyone who truly and thoroughly understands the game of football, Joel Stephens is not only the *best* player in Section IV, he is the *best* player in New York State."

It was not until three years later, when Scot attended Joel's wake and sent an eye-catching arrangement of blue and gold flowers, that our differences were put behind us.

Ironically, Scot later lost his beautiful two-year old daughter, Alexandra, in a car accident.

The awards and honors kept coming in, and Joel was informed that he had been named to the "Schutt Manufacturing Top 100 All-American Team" announced in *USA Today*. This is an independent rating service and evaluation of high school football talent and skill across the United States. Joel, although honored and flattered to receive these awards, was intelligent enough to understand that the most important thing was his academics, something that he could always revert back to for him to be successful in the future. He told the sportswriters that he was grateful to win them because he felt they were a tribute not just to him, but to our football team, all of our players, and our coaching staff. He said, "Sports are important, but the more important thing is my education. I have received a good education at Notre Dame, and these awards reflect that."

The award that Joel cherished the most was the celebrated and esteemed "Ernie Davis Award." This tribute was much more than just a football honor. It was a recognition voted on by a committee headed by Marty Harrigan, a retired Marine and principal at Elmira Free Academy. Marty was a Syracuse alumnus, Ernie's high school football coach, and the person most instrumental in Ernie attending Syracuse University and playing football for the Orangemen. Davis was the first African-American to win the Heisman Trophy. This honor goes to the most outstanding college football player in the country. Mr. Harrigan was a legendary, old-fashioned administrator whose hands on approach to discipline was sometimes taken literally by this diminutive, cigar smoking, arthritic tough as nails Irishmen. Also on the committee were the five area high school football coaches, and a panel of gentlemen who knew of the late Ernie Davis' humanitarian and charitable works. This honor is bestowed on an individual from the metro Elmira area who demonstrates outstanding skill and abilities on the football field, but more importantly, someone who is a credit to his team, coaches, school, family, and community in all his endeavors.

Chapter 16

Similarities between Joel Stephens and Ernie Davis

Ernie Davis was a legend from coast to coast because he was a remarkable young man who displayed courage and strength in the face of misfortune, and whose exploits on the gridiron were well chronicled. He was an extraordinary man who had to deal with racism and later terminal, acute monocytic leukemia which ended his dream of playing in the National Football League.

During my childhood, I was fortunate enough to live a few blocks from the late Ernie Davis. I recall him being larger than life and I often reflect on how he treated every one of us in the neighborhood. He endlessly threw the football to our group as we ran undisciplined patterns. He bought us hard candy from the local stores and shared his lunches with those less fortunate. He tossed us in the air with those big hands, not one of us ever scared that this giant would fumble or misplay us. Ernie Davis was a special human being. If you had the opportunity to meet him once in your life, you felt fortunate.

Joel's story followed the same path as that of Ernie Davis. Both of these gentlemen extended themselves to a variety of people in a very gracious and generous manner. They were heroes who inspired so many before eventually being struck down in their prime, both dying in their early twenties (Joel at twenty-two, Ernie at twenty-three). Each remained positive despite grim circumstances. There was never any bitterness, or anger, or resentment, or blaming others. There was no wavering in their faith in their God, thinking of others first, right to the end. As sick and ailing as these two men were, their contagious smiles and their once-strong bodies that had betrayed them, still resonated strength, vigor, and vitality to all whom they met. History says that Ernie's doctors kept his diagnosis away from him for as long as they could. Joel Stephens declined to discuss his prognosis. However, both families and immediate friends knew deep down that the physicians probably did not encourage much hope in either case.

Their tragic fates some thirty-five years apart, parallel each other in other ways as well. Ernie and Joel both came from Pennsylvania, Ernie moving to Elmira from the Pittsburgh area at a young age. Both were exceptional in three sports: football, basketball, and baseball. Both achieved high school All-American status in two sports, and both died ten months after they were diagnosed with cancer. Ernie and Joel had smiles as big as the state of New York and loved to help people, especially young people. They never allowed hard times or their deteriorating health to change them. They were both loved and admired by countless thousands, not for the way they played sports, but because of the way they conducted themselves, each having the ability to break down barriers among people. They influenced people from coast to coast, carrying with them the blueprint and a torch, lighting the way for all of us to follow. They were super heroes who felt that they could help the world. How could you not root for them? All the goodness that they offered to others was always free. They never expected anything in return. They did it because it made others, as well as themselves, feel good. It is easy to behave righteously when someone is watching. It is how you act when you think that nobody is observing that is truly the test of one's character. It never mattered to them. They always showed their character, and never acted like one. Even when their time was winding down, they both kept a positive outlook on life, never fading, weakening, and never giving in, either mentally or spiritually.

Joel, upon receiving the Ernie Davis Award in 1995, stated for the record, "Now winning this award with Ernie's name on it, I from here on out, hold myself to an even higher standard."

This is the photo used as a guide to sculpt his statue to be placed in a memorial park at Notre Dame High School in Elmira, New York.

Chapter 17

The Crusader Classic and Myrtle Beach

Joel's final basketball season began in November of 1994 and he was never close to feeling 100% until well into the following January. The pounding and grueling football schedule had taken a toll on his frame, but to his credit, he never missed a practice or game throughout his high school career. Not having a dominating center, we were expected to be competitive, but far from a dominant hardwood force. Joel was an excellent player who could rebound, defend, handle the ball versus pressure, shoot the three, and take the ball with authority to the basket. There were not too many brave enough to step in his path to take a charge, or try to stop him from getting to the front of the rim. He was strong inside, wide, and with leaping ability that allowed him to play bigger than his 6'2" stature.

I recall on one occasion when the bus was to leave at 4:30 p.m. sharp for a game against Corning East. The players knew that the bus was departing on time whether you were there or not. It made no difference where you fell on the depth chart; there were no special privileges. It was time to leave and Joel was not seated in his usual position in the last row on the back of the bus. Trying to treat everyone the same, I instructed the bus driver to embark on our destination, minus Joel. As we were rounding the corner of the school's driveway, Joel came speeding in with his arms flailing, trying to motion the bus to stop. "Keep going," I told the bus driver as Joel turned and followed the bus for the next twenty miles. The team entered the gym with Joel in very close proximity. He came scurrying over to me to apologize for being late, and I accepted it. However, I told him that he would sit out the first half, a sentence that I knew would seem an eternity to him. Joel reminded me that one of his high school goals was to be an "Iron Man" and never miss a start during his varsity career in football, basketball, or baseball. I replied, "Then get a new goal because that one has now ended." "But coach," he insisted, "I was just a few minutes late," to which I countered, "I noticed that you haven't been late for any of your tanning appointments." He shrugged those big, broad shoulders, laughed and accepted his punishment. Joel had been going to tanning sessions to prepare for his trip to Myrtle Beach, South Carolina after the Crusader Classic Christmas Tournament, and as a treatment of a skin condition that was still bothering him. Joel was inserted into the lineup in the third quarter; he torched the nets for 23-second half points, thus sealing a Notre Dame come-from-behind victory. Thank God for reason taking over my better judgment and not sitting him the entire game. I recall Joel's dad being quiet after the game, but his mother was 100% supportive of my decision to discipline him.

Next up for the hoopsters was our Crusader Classic Invitational Basketball Tournament, then in its sixth year. We opened with Bishop Walsh out of Williamsport, and Addison played against Mansfield in the preliminary contest. If all went as planned, Addison with their 6'7" superstar and outstanding guard, John Works, would square off against our team, led by Joel Stephens. The championship game lived up to its billing and it seemed neither team played any defense. John Works was everything we thought he was, and so was Joel. The game ended tied in regulation, and it was the same after the first overtime. During the second overtime period, Works sliced and diced his way for a reverse, two-handed jam that sent his team into the lead, 76-74 with 12 seconds left to play. Our 5'8" point guard, Mike Lynch, took a shot with six seconds left on the clock and it caromed in and out, and then out of bounds off of one of their players underneath our basket. With four seconds left to play, Mike Berrettini put the ball inbounds and hit Joel gliding away from our goal, leading him to the deep, baseline corner. As quickly as Joel caught the inbounds pass, he twisted and contorted his body, flicked his wrist, and let go an arching rainbow of a shot. He then proceeded to fall into our student Basketball Crazies seated in the stands. The three-point shot found nothing but net, earning us the Tournament Championship. John Works had a great game, scoring 37 points in a losing cause, and Joel wound up with 29 points. Works and Stephens had put on a dazzling display of athleticism for the standing room only crowd in the sweltering Notre Dame gymnasium. After the game, Joel made a rare request. He wondered if he could have a basketball and I flipped him one from our opened ball rack. I thought he might want to take it over break to hone his round ball skills, or to work on some shooting drills. As I tossed him the ball, he said, "No coach, I mean the game ball." People who know me understand that I am fanatical about routine, and very superstitious in my game rituals. We had just won a big tournament and I did not want to be separated from my "binky." To give Joel a ball was one thing. To give him the game ball from a winning contest was a huge request, one that would be a big sacrifice in my eyes.

Joel informed me that a five-year-old fan who had recently been diagnosed with leukemia was in attendance on that evening. This ball was special and Joel wanted the team to sign it and date it in hopes that it would bring comfort to this youngster. It might even bring some good fortune. Joel never dwelled on what tomorrow might bring. His main focus was in "Who" brought tomorrow, and he knew "Who" was always in control. People were milling in the gym, waiting for the votes to be cast and tabulated for the all tournament team, and for the MVP. As expected, Joel won the MVP and proceeded to walk towards the scorer's table where this pale, sickly youngster was seated with his family. No one in the gym knew of Joel's intentions and without any fanfare, he whispered words of encouragement into the sick lad's ear, and gave him not only the autographed ball, but his MVP trophy as well. As he left the boy's side, he gave him an affectionate tap on his head, trying to reassure him that everything was going to be all right. This boy, Patrick Sullivan, has now been cancer free for the past 12 years. He decided to attend Notre Dame High School, has done very well in the classroom, and he has been a key contributor as a starter on the football, basketball, and the lacrosse teams. Ironically, he was named a recipient of the Joel Andrew Stephens 5 C Award in 2009.

After that game, a group of twelve friends planned to leave the school's parking lot and head for a four day golfing trip that would also involve watching games at the Myrtle Beach Basketball Classic. This tournament is the premier high school tournament in the country, bringing in many of the top twenty-five teams across the nation. Joel and another player, Brian Murray, asked if they could follow the group, just to watch basketball and to get away. It was okay with their families and we included them in our pack. Immediately following this emotional scene, the time had come for our 850 mile trip south through the night. It would be a bit more enjoyable knowing that we repeated as our tournament's champions. Helping to pack people's vans, I watched one of my friends hit a snag when he went to grab Joel's duffle bag. "What the hell do you have in here, a body?" muttered Steve Snyder. Once we all heard the clang, we realized that the sound was about 150 pounds of free weights that Joel packed so he would not miss a day of lifting. I told Joel that I would pay for a week's membership at Gold's Gym in North Myrtle if he would leave the weights in our wrestling room. He agreed and we were off.

Brian Murray, Joel's teammate, good friend, and an excellent golfer with a two handicap, was Joel's driving companion. I did not see much of Joel, except at the basketball games, and occasionally he would stop by my room and chat for a while. He usually was lifting, running the beach, watching games, or eating. We had a great four days, and the adults commented on Joel's mature behavior when he was with us during evening dinners, and at the Myrtle Beach Convention Center, watching the top high school talent in the country.

On our return home, a senior girl who was not one of the so-called "cool kids" of her class asked Joel if he would like to go to the Winter Fling formal dance as her escort. I was within earshot of the conversation and marveled at how quickly Joel said that he would be happy to go. I just thought how classy, caring, and thoughtful my friend was, knowing that he would never want to hurt anyone's feelings by saying no. He understood that rejection could be the greatest form of hurt, and he never wanted to do that to anyone. He did not just understand it; he lived it. He bought her a corsage, took her to dinner, and by all accounts, showed her a great time. But then again, that was what people expected from Joel, and what he certainly expected from himself. His sole purpose in life was to be a difference maker, and a difference maker in a positive way. He did have an addiction, a craving. It wasn't alcohol, or drugs, or sex. It was a compulsion to make others feel wanted and important.

The basketball team tied for the division title and with Joel leading the charge, we went untested through the first three games of sectionals. It was very likely we would face Deposit in the finals at the Broome County Arena. I had been scouting them as often as possible, trying to get some insight on their players. The Lumberjacks were composed of basically 10 to 12 new players who were not on the prior year's roster. About six months earlier, a community of approximately 100 Muslim families uprooted from New York City and moved to the outskirts of Deposit. Many of these boys were very good basketball players, with a blend of height and quickness that made them go from mediocre to very talented. It didn't help that we came out and our shooting was colder than the hockey ice underneath the hardwood floor. We needed to play probably better than what we were capable of, but we hung in with them, always maintaining a 6-10 point deficit, keeping it respectable. What impressed many that evening was the effort Joel gave at both ends of the court. I knew deep down that he probably wanted to be at baseball practice which had started earlier. It is my philosophy not to let players practice another sport when the in-season sport is still in session. Even though we were down by ten with fifty seconds to play and with little hope to win, Joel kept throwing his body into metal chairs, which lined the court, and into anything else that was between him and gaining possession of the ball. As much as he wanted to begin baseball, he despised losing even more. Joel wanted to come out on top, but more important to Joel was that his effort always be the best.

Chapter 18

Joel's Amateur Baseball Career

Joel's three years of varsity baseball at Notre Dame were spectacular most of the time, but turned somewhat lackluster during his senior year. That was mainly due to the fact that coaches in the area just opted not to pitch to him, beginning the proverbial unintentional, intentional pass. Despite this, Joel was a lifetime .400 hitter, and led the area in every offensive and defensive category. After his junior season, Joel was selected to play on the National Junior Olympic Team in St. Louis, Missouri. He was the starting left fielder, often sending balls out of Busch Stadium over a two-week span. It was at this time that he really drew the attention of college and pro scouts. In November of 1994, Joel made an official visit to Clemson University, the number one pre-season baseball team in the nation at the time. On his return, Joel told me that he had decided to pursue his baseball career, and that he signed an early letter of intent to play for Jack Leggett and the Division I Clemson Tigers. Joel was excited about playing for this perennial baseball power, traditionally ranked in the top 20 in the country every year. It is a program that has put numerous players in the major leagues, and that was further incentive for Joel to enroll. Tim Corbin, an assistant coach at Clemson, was in Elmira for the signing of the national letter of intent, and suggested that Joel would only continue to get better once he started to play and concentrate on baseball all year round. Joel was on cloud nine, knowing that he would be going south to an excellent academic institution, to an excellent baseball program, and to a school that had great facilities, a great coaching staff, and a great group of returning players. We put together a signing breakfast party held at our school, inviting the media, Joel's coaches, and other close family and friends who were influential in Joel's success. Over 25 major college football programs were recruiting Joel, but the gridiron's loss was Clemson University's gain.

During the 1995 spring baseball season, many professional baseball scouts came to observe Joel swing a bat, or time him running to first base. It was not uncommon to see 10 to 15 scouts taking their stances along the fences, or sitting in the bleachers an hour before game time. They felt that if opposing teams did not give him a pitch to hit, at least watching him taking batting practice was the next best option. Many times, I took Joel and a few players out on the ball field during their free time and let the scouts take a look at Joel swinging the bat. I was standing in left center field of Notre Dame's diamond, shagging balls for Joel. For a time, I was backed up to the fence, some 340 feet away from home plate. I realized at some point during these sessions that it would have been more appropriate to stand on the opposite side of the fence because that was where two out of every three swings were landing. Scouts wondered if they would lose a draft choice if they opted to draft this talent, and he still attended Clemson. All I knew was that every scout was impressed when Joel put down the aluminum bat and walked up to the batter's box with a wooden bat in his hand, something he would have to do to play professional baseball. Joel was the only person I knew in the area who had the strength to navigate a wooden weapon through the strike zone, faster than others could put a knife into a $40 steak. Joel was named to the All USA High School All-American Baseball Team, and was drafted in the 9th round by the Baltimore Orioles. In a microwave society where everyone wants everything yesterday, Joel set goals early on in his life, and diligently worked at attaining them. Most look for the quick way to Easy Street. Not Joel Stephens. Joel was an example of what can happen to people who are genuinely good, and who work hard.

Chapter 19

The Baseball Minor Leagues

After Joel's high school graduation in 1995, he reported to the Baltimore Orioles Class A farm team in Bluefield, West Virginia. It took Joel a few weeks to get adjusted to a new environment, and to an upgrade in the level of competition. He was their starting left fielder, batting fifth in the lineup. Night after night, he showed promise and talent with a .280 batting average, as well as power to all fields. When I had talked with some of the scouts who were interested in drafting Joel a few months earlier, many expressed their belief that he had a very good shot at a major league career in three to five years because of his strength, the lift he could get on the ball, and his quickness. It was exciting to realize that Notre Dame High School had one of its alumni playing professional baseball and doing well. To Joel, this was a lifelong dream, but one that wasn't about the glory, but rather about doing what he wanted to be doing and moving forward in his life. Playing in this rural town of Bluefield, Joel befriended other minor leaguers who would go on to the big show. Ryan Minor, a first team All-American basketball player from Oklahoma, and who replaced Cal Ripken Jr. at third base, was Joel's roommate. David Dellucci (Padres, Yankees, and Indians) and Doug DeCinces Jr. (son of the former major leaguer of the same name), were two of his best friends. Joel called about once a week to keep Jayne and me up to date on what was happening, and I shared with him the latest on football practices and games.

I recall the week of the Tioga game. They were a scary and intimidating squad, returning everyone except their quarterback. This was the same team that had dismantled us the prior year and I vowed early in the summer that we would prepare like never before to get a win in this rematch. As a staff, we never try to fuel any fires for our opponents with predictions, quotes, or frivolous guarantees about the outcome of a game. This game was a completely different story. I could not help but remember when the Tioga assistant coach had undervalued our high school star a year earlier. I don't believe that one can justify speaking of high school kids to reporters in a negative manner. Many players, coaches, fans, and even my parents didn't give us a chance of winning this game. When Joel called, I announced with confidence in my voice, "We will win this game!" He had been around me long enough to know that I usually paint gloomy pictures of the future, but deep down, I think differently. We try to go into games thinking we are primed to win. I heard Jayne tell him, "I don't know, Joel. He keeps saying they are prepared, and they are going to win." I think our quarterback at the time was worried about confronting the Tioga Tigers. I am sure he was not alone in recalling the previous year's humiliation. On my way to the game that Friday, I made an illegal U-turn on the parkway and went back to my house, frantically searching for the tape of last year's game. Articles of five of our wins against Tioga in the last six years lined the locker room walls with our quotes, and Joel's quotes highlighted in orange magic marker. We did nothing but praise the Tigers program and their players. In my pre-game remarks, I told my team that this rivalry had gotten personal because they made negative comments about one of our players. We talked about respect for others, and especially about respect for our prior year's star. Saying something negative about Joel Stephens put a big bull's eye on their jerseys for forty-eight minutes. I guaranteed that the outcome would be different, but deep down, I wasn't so sure.

The players were seated in our traditional horseshoe fashion, and one could hear a pin drop. Every player was so intense, focused, and all had white knuckles from clenching their fists so hard. There was no letdown on that night, and they did it for Joel. With Notre Dame scoring 30 unanswered points, there was no question who was the better team.

Joel's high school football career comes to an end as he walks off the field for the final time.

When I returned home, there were numerous calls left on my answering machine, several of them from Joel wondering about the final outcome. Later in the week, the team received a note from Joel, saying how proud of them he was, and congratulating them on preparing so well. He would be home shortly from West Virginia and he was excited about taking in a game and seeing everyone.

Chapter 20

The Delmarva Shorebirds

In Joel's second year of minor league baseball, he was assigned to the Delmarva Shorebirds, a Baltimore Orioles Class "A" farm team located in Salisbury, MD. This team and stadium was owned and operated by one of the country's chicken entrepreneurs, Frank Perdue. Joel told us stories of Mr. Perdue's house and of having the best chicken dinners he ever tasted. Chicken was Joel's favorite dish. Jayne and I were thrilled with the location of Joel's new team because it was only 35 minutes from Fenwick Island, a beach we have been vacationing at twice a year since our honeymoon in 1989. During the last week of June, we invited my nephews and some of their friends to join us for some R-and-R for a few days. One of the boys on this mini-getaway was Andy Agan, the son of the man who would later be instrumental in flying Joel home from the West Coast during his final days. All of us wanted to surprise Joel prior to his evening game. That afternoon, we went to the motel and knocked on his door. He was surprised and excited to see us, but Jayne noticed an emptiness in his eyes. Despite having so many friends, I was taken aback that he was sitting on his efficiency room floor, alone and just off somewhere else. Reflecting back on it now, I think he was not feeling well and probably worried that something was seriously wrong. He was humbled by the fact that we had traveled eight hours to watch him play, take him to dinner, and spend some time with him, reminiscing about the old days. That evening during the game, he hit three lasers, two of them for extra bases, and he scored the winning run. Joel had chosen his future and that was to be a professional baseball player. To no one's surprise, no matter what role he chose, he always did it well.

On our journey back home, something just didn't feel right. Joel looked drained and worried about something, but he did not let that dampen our good time. Just before we boarded the minivan to head back home, Joel gave me a big hug and said that he was contemplating a possible return to college to play Division I football. This caught me off guard, but I later thought that it was probably just a passing feeling. Jayne, myself, and Jayne's sister Elizabeth were returning to Maryland in a few weeks for a longer stay, and I would be able to have a heart-to-heart discussion with Joel, and ascertain if he was serious about this career change. The Shorebirds were playing well and were winning their division, most likely heading to the playoffs at the end of August. Joel was going on an extended road trip with the team, returning in time to meet us once again at the beach.

We had plenty of room at the beach house that we were renting and invited Joel to spend time with us after his practices and games. He jumped at the chance to have some home-cooked meals, casual conversations, and to walk the beach without a care in the world. Elizabeth, who has Down's Syndrome, in all of her candid, natural, and unrestrained innocence, just adored Joel. It wasn't that Joel's muscles were tighter than two coats of paint, but rather because of his loving and caring nature, and all the attention he showered on her. It was a beautiful picture, watching the two of them stroll down the beach, the blazing sun scorching their skin, hand in hand, kicking the water as it came crashing to the shore. Who knows what they were talking about as they paraded out of sight. I do know that Joel could have dated just about anyone he wanted, but he was content spending time with Elizabeth, making her feel that she was "America's Next Top Model."

That evening Joel had a game, and the three of us were his guests. We made plans to go to dinner after the game. Little did we know that the seventy-five people hanging around the clubhouse entrance well after the final out were there waiting to get Joel's autograph, and to speak to him. I don't recall seeing any males in this group of enthusiasts, but I do recall that many of them were mesmerized by his politeness, and his graciousness. An elderly lady handed Joel a picture of her 25-year-old niece, with her address and phone number on the back, with the directive to give her a call. A single mom, probably in her late thirties, gave Joel a plate of homemade oatmeal cookies. She then invited him over for dinner later in the week, and mentioned that he wouldn't be disappointed. Time passed and the only light left on at the stadium was hovering over Joel and his female entourage. My empty stomach was making more noise than the sound of the cars racing at the Daytona 500 so I reminded Joel that we had dinner reservations and that we were almost an hour late as it was. When Joel was ready to leave, all seekers had gotten their autographs, pictures, and conversation. Joel then quietly excused himself. The next day, Joel and I were watching old football tapes as the ladies headed towards the white sand of the beach. This was the time Joel picked to discuss playing on the gridirons once again. He explained to me that he was tired of living out of a suitcase, and that he wanted to get a college degree and eventually become a teacher and coach. He wanted to meet a nice girl, not the "Baseball Annies" that showed up at games. He loved the idea of having "little Joels" or maybe "Joelettes." He dreamed of watching them take their first step, eating their first Oreo cookie and getting that chocolate goop all over their face. He wanted his children to have the opportunity to be influenced by his parents and his grandparents on both sides of the family. Someone once said that Joel was so straight, he could sleep in a three-piece suit for 8 hours and never get it wrinkled. I didn't know if that was possible but I did know that Joel Stephens was honest, straightforward, and sincere. With this decision, Joel felt that he was giving up on something and that he was letting some people down. I asked him who. He said, "People like you and Jayne." I reminded him of what Rodney Dangerfield said, "Always look out for Number 1, and make sure you don't step in Number 2." I added, "I know you don't live your life with you as your first and only priority, but in this instance, you have to do what your heart tells you is right."

Reflecting back, I think he wanted a son or daughter that he could spend time with, even if only for a while. He knew his body better than anyone else, and I think he was realizing that it was betraying him, and telling him something was drastically wrong.

When we returned to Elmira, I happened to come in contact with David Walker, the running backs' coach for Syracuse University. I casually mentioned that I just spent some time with Joel Stephens and that he was toying with the possibility of leaving professional baseball, setting his sights on getting a college education, and playing big-time football. If Joel played college football, he wanted to do it for the Syracuse Orangemen. There were very strong ties between Elmira, Marty Harrigan who helped recruit Joel for Syracuse when he was in high school, and the legendary, Ernie Davis. David was so excited that he wanted to call Joel immediately, but I asked him to hold off until baseball playoffs were finished, and I had one more chance to see if Joel was truly serious about his decision. David Walker, who is a class act, always thought very highly of Joel and he agreed to work with us anyway he could.

The Shorebirds made the playoffs and they won the league title. During their title stretch, Joel called periodically to say that he had been doing fine at the plate and in the field. After one of his games, however, I asked him how he did, and he told me that he had some pain in his back, so the coaches scratched him from the starting line-up. After I hung up, I told my wife that I had just heard a first. Joel Stephens had admitted that he was in some pain. This surprised me because Joel was one of the toughest guys I ever knew. He was tough physically, mentally, and spiritually. With her woman's intuition, Jayne feared that something was going on with him. I told her that he was fine, probably swinging too hard and pulled a muscle. Joel visited a doctor a few days later, who looking at a strapping 22-year-old professional athlete, also diagnosed it as a pulled muscle.

Chapter 21

Joel's Return from Baseball

Unbeknownst to Joel, I had been in contact for a month with David Walker and Paul Pasqualoni. Coach "P" was the head coach of Syracuse University. He felt as if he knew Joel, viewing tapes given to him by one of our former players, Bob Grosvenor. Coach Walker inquired about Joel's fitness, since he had not played any football for over two years. I told David, "Remember, he has been playing professional baseball since high school, not sitting in some saloon, playing pool, and you will see for yourself when we all meet." Joel returned in October and made a quick stop at our house before heading home. I hoped that he would not be too disappointed with me, but I informed him that I had been in conversations with the coaches from Syracuse. Talk about a smile from ear to ear, this young man had it, and he was ready to take the next steps to complete the recruiting process.

He had gone through the same stress a few years prior, but the second time around was still exciting for him. Joel looked a little thinner to me than the last time we met, and I asked him what he weighed. He said he was around 222 pounds, down about 8 pounds from a month ago. I just chalked up his weight loss to the fact he had been playing ball during the hot, summer months, and that was sure to take its toll.

Within a week, Joel, David Walker, and I met in my office at Notre Dame High School. David and I were seated when Joel arrived. He was wearing a white, under-armour t-shirt that outlined his physique pretty well. Coach Walker and Joel exchanged greetings with Joel calling him by name. He tried to do this because he felt that it showed people he cared enough to remember who they were, once he had met you. David gave a glance my way and I understood his wink that said to me, "What a physical specimen! How could I have asked if he kept himself in shape?"

Prior to Joel coming home, he went to Hawaii and then to the Tampa Bay area with a few friends, just to wind down from his grueling baseball season. Naturally, while in Florida, Joel did not take any time off from lifting, working out with many of the elite athletes in the Bay area. Syracuse heavily recruits the state of Florida. Joel knew many of the Orange players living on the Gulf Coast, and he also had met some of those who had just committed to play for Coach Pasqualoni. Walker and Joel talked for two hours. Joel never realized at the time that he might have been lifting with some of his future teammates. Three days later, Syracuse offered Joel a full scholarship.

Chapter 22

Joel Attends Syracuse / West Virginia Game

Joel had an innate ability to connect with people, and he accepted them with their strengths as well as with their faults and vulnerabilities. He was a deep thinker who always explored every option before coming to a final decision. If he ever found himself in a hole, he would stop digging, and find another way to proceed. He understood that hard work was crucial for success and that success had to be earned, not simply asked for and received. All of his dedication and perseverance had once again paid off for this gentle man. He prayed hard and he prayed often, but always he prayed for others and their intentions as well as his own. My family prayed hard for Joel, and then we learned that he was awarded a free college education and a chance to play football close to home. As soon as his acceptance was finalized, he informed Peter Angelos, the owner of the Baltimore Orioles, that he would not return to baseball the following season.

We were invited to attend a Syracuse football game as guests of the coaches at the college. Joel, Jayne and I had a nice, relaxing 90-mile ride to the game, with me wanting to stop at every fast food restaurant along the way. Joel asked me, "Coach, is there any food that you don't like?" I said, "Yeah, beets, and knock off the wisecracks." He said he would, but he added that he felt that a doctor would make my colon into a semicolon after my next ulcer. From the opening kickoff, Joel's eyes were glued to the astro turf, and I would guess that he didn't say ten sentences during the four quarters. It wasn't that he was being unsociable or standoffish. It simply was that he was very focused on watching the action. That was Joel – learning, studying, and analyzing every football play at every opportunity. Happiness was something Joel may have finally attained.

After the game, we were invited down to the locker room area where the coaching staff and recruitment coordinators rolled out the red carpet for Joel. They made all of us feel comfortable, but they especially made Joel feel welcome, knowing that he would soon be wearing the orange and blue.

I remember having a conversation on our trip home from the game. We were traveling in a Cadillac that had plenty of legroom in both the front and back seats. Joel was a front seat passenger, and Jayne was stretched out, beginning to quickly doze off in the back seat. Over and over again throughout the first hour, Joel seemed unusually fidgety, and he was unable to get comfortable. I asked him if he needed to find a rest stop, and he said, "No. That pulled muscle in my back still hurts and I wish it would go away." I explained to him that pulled muscles do not last 4 months, or take that long to heal. I suggested that he now see a specialist and I recommended that he do it soon. Jayne joined our conversation and as one who worked in the medical field, she was listening attentively to every word. I recall asking him if he was taking anything to try to alleviate his pain. He told us he was taking Advil and Ibuprofen for the past 10 to 12 weeks and neither seemed to help. I asked him either "how many?" or "how often?" The red flag immediately went flying as soon as he told us that he took 20 to 24 pills a day on a pretty regular basis. Jayne made Joel promise that he would make an appointment with a gastroenterologist the next day. Joel promised he would.

Joel and his family got the earliest appointment available, which was in ten days. In the interim, our school once again was pitted against the boys from Walton High School and playing for the Sectional Championship. On that day, we took a good whipping playing on a muddy, rain-soaked field in Binghamton. Their 230-pound linemen had a great deal more traction and stability in these conditions than our 175-pound linemen.   I recall seeing my dad talking to Joel at the entrance gate just before the opening kickoff. Later that evening, my father mentioned to me that he didn't think Joel's color looked very good. Now if my father, not a high sensate by any stretch of the imagination, had noticed this graying hue, then I really began to worry about what was going on in his body that people were missing. My dad's observation unfortunately proved to be prophetic.

Chapter 23

Joel's First Doctor's Visit

The pain in Joel's back hadn't subsided so Joyce Stephens made an appointment with Dr. John Rominger who is an outstanding gastroenterologist in our area. Dr. Rominger scheduled a colonoscopy for Joel at St. Joseph's Hospital to see if the problem was related to his abdomen instead of his back. His parents, Jayne, and I accompanied him and we were in the waiting room when Dr. Rominger greeted us after the 45 minute procedure. He explained what he had done, and what he had found. He said that there was something obstructing Joel's colon, and that he had been unable to get the G-I tube past a certain point. He was not certain about a diagnosis but took biopsies of surrounding tissue. He met with the Stephens a week later and recommended that Joel's problem be researched more thoroughly with more advanced tests and scans. Dr. Rominger and his partner, Dr. Bruno Mazza, were well aware of who Joel Stephens was, and that he was soon going to sign a letter of intent to play football on a full scholarship to Syracuse University. Dr. Mazza had been Jim Boeheim's (Syracuse University Hall of Fame Basketball Coach) roommate and teammate on the golf team for four years in college. Dr. Rominger suggested that it could be heavy scar tissue built up in the intestines, possibly from some type of Crohn's disease.

The Stephens family returned to Pennsylvania, with Joel, Jayne, and myself going back to our house. After dinner, Joel called his dad and asked if Syracuse had contacted him. David Walker, not knowing any of Joel's health issues, had been expected to give him a call later that day to discuss Joel's signing date. I overheard Joel speaking with his dad, "I have to tell them, dad. If they withdraw the scholarship because of what I have, I will work even harder as a walk-on, forcing them to eventually reinstate it."

Joel hung up and sat in our recliner for a few moments, putting himself into deep thought. Joel always thought before he spoke, and he did it on this occasion as well. He never wanted to hurt anyone or say the wrong thing. Even though Joel was speaking out loud, deep down, he really was speaking to himself. He understood why his dad was very concerned and did not want him to tell Syracuse that he might have Crohn's disease. He was also telling himself that he just did not operate like that. He needed to inform Syracuse, and he wanted to be completely above board with the doctor's opinion. No determination had been made in confirming any illness at all. Joel asked me what he should do and I said, "I understand where your dad is coming from, but you have to do what makes you feel comfortable." Jayne and myself are no doctors, but Joel asked us, "What is Crohn's disease?" I told him that it is a condition for which you have to almost abuse your body to a certain degree. You have to start eating like me, reverting to a diet full of fats, grease, oils, and other non-roughage items. I wasn't sure if that was Crohn's or diverticulitis. Joel was upset as I continued the list. I also told him that I knew of professional athletes playing at that time with the disease, and even Syracuse's starting tight end, Chris Gedney, had been diagnosed with Crohn's. As they watched television, Joel and Jayne talked for a while about everything from a girl that Joel had been dating in Maryland to which actresses and actors had cosmetic surgeries. When he left that evening, he was clearly still upset. I don't think that he thought what was ailing him would be fatal. What alarmed him was how long was it going to take for him to feel well enough to begin college. He wanted to begin in January so that he could get a few courses under his belt, and he would be able to train and get more acquainted with some of the coaches and experienced players. He also wanted to begin to learn his new school's complex football system. However, the news just kept spiraling downhill.

Abraham Lincoln once said that when we are born, we are given three names: the last name we inherit, the first name our parents give us, and finally, the name we make for ourselves. Joel had already done a superior job with this latter one, but he was not finished. The way that Joel handled his misfortune enabled him to achieve even greater heights, creating an even larger legacy.

Chapter24

Joel's First Surgery

CAT scans revealed that Joel Stephens had some type of mass in his colon.

Dr. Robert Huddle, an experienced and well-respected surgeon, was chosen to perform the operation. Dr. Huddle's dad and brother are also surgeons and Joel was in capable hands. Dr. Huddle had been a standout cross-country runner at Notre Dame University, and he understood how important this operation was, especially for a fellow athlete. He promised to do his best to get Joel back to being Joel. I do recall Dr. Huddle speaking to the Stephens family. After a very lengthy operation, he felt that he removed most of the baseball size tumor, along with three inches of his intestines, and part of his colon. Tissue samples had to be sent to the lab for further analysis to determine if it was cancerous. He did say that it was "very ugly" and that in his twenty years of performing surgeries, he had never run across anything of that nature. I wasn't hoping for good luck, but rather, I was praying very hard that Joel did not have bad luck. It didn't sound positive to me, but we were determined to pray hard until the results came back.

The report came back and it wasn't good news. It was cancer and it was a very aggressive type. It presented more than a formidable opponent for Joel. That "Eureka" moment when someone would tell us that all would be fine never came. Everyone was devastated, everyone that is, but Joel. Joel always believed in the hereafter, but he also believed in the here and now. Even presented with this terrible news, Joel embraced it with optimism. Joel told me that he didn't view this as a final chapter to his life, but rather an opening to accomplish greater things. A person has sole power to manage his thoughts and feelings throughout a regular day. His demeanor and psyche never wavered upon hearing this bad news. Joel, the architect and author of what was to unfold, made his mind up he was going to stay positive, and his song would be one of resolve and determination. He only wanted to know what was the next course of action, and what he had to do to give himself a chance. I know I was questioning everything in life, including my faith in God. Joel's diagnosis was real. It was not a game of stickball where you could have "do-overs." Instead of people aiding and helping Joel, it would be Joel extending his love and comfort to others in this most perilous of times. "Coach D, I have a lot to think about, but nothing to worry about. I also don't want you and Jayne worrying about me either. I will be fine." His courage was inspiring. Joel believed in God's love, and he introduced God to many others through his strength and his actions in the difficult days ahead.

The bad news circulated throughout the Twin Tiers as fast as Joel blew by a headline with his name in it. This was mainly due to an article the local newspaper decided to print about this turn of events. I know there are benefits as well as drawbacks in being a high-profile athlete. I just felt that in this case, a few courtesies could have been granted, and patient confidentiality could have been honored. A local sportswriter decided to get "the scoop" by misleading Joel's elderly grandmother. The news was going to leak eventually because in Elmira, everyone is either related to someone, or they are friends with someone who knows something. Joel had just come out of major surgery, and the hospital was bombarded with well-wishers and curiosity seekers, all trying to express their concern and support. Prior to visiting hours, Joel tried to power walk around the nurse's station to keep his body and mind as physically fit as possible for the long road ahead. Roughly 200 people visited Joel over several days, and he made everyone feel welcomed and wanted. He was raised by a caring family, a family who taught him to always say "please," "thank you," " have a nice day" or "you're welcome." Some people stayed only long enough to wish him prayers, while others never knew when to leave. He was always kind, maybe too kind. His body had been heavily taxed, but tired and exhausted, he still felt responsible to entertain his visitors.

Chapter 25

The News Gets Worse

Joel was larger than life in the eyes of many. He was as tough as foundry-forged steel, but this new enemy wasn't going to be denied. About two weeks after the first operation, Joel was once again having severe abdominal pain. Dr. Huddle, hoping that perhaps that there was a kink in the colon, or that an abscess had developed, scheduled emergency surgery.

I recall hearing the news at school and asked the principal for permission to visit Joel in the hospital. Traveling over the bridge of the Chemung River, I spotted a car moving in the opposite direction with two of my former players who were close friends of Joel. They just shook their heads as we passed on opposite sides of the double yellow line. My gut told me that John Maio and Damian Saks had just left the hospital and that they had been on their way to give me the bad news.

As I arrived at the hospital, I found the Stephens family and Dr. Huddle in discussion about the surgery. This time, the adversary was not a minor problem as originally thought. It was the same ugly foe that had reared its head two weeks earlier. The tumor had almost completely returned, more forceful and antagonistic as ever. My reaction was to think that they would just take it out again. Joel was strong, Joel was a competitor, and Joel would prevail. Dr. Huddle tried his best to explain to the family that when the cancer grows back that quickly, it is basically saying that it can't be beaten, no matter who you are. For the next nine months, Joel never asked why. I did enough of that for both of us. I thought, "This cannot be happening. He has so much going for him. He has so much potential. Please Lord, don't do this!" All I was asking for was just one more victory, one more triumph, as Joel lay quietly resting in the recovery room.

Joel's mom recalled walking into his room one evening after the diagnosis and starting to cry as she watched her son sleeping. She felt so helpless and hated to think of life without her Joel. He woke to the sounds of his mom's sobs and reassured her that everything was going to be OK. He said, "Mom, you know I have always been a religious person, and that I believe strongly in God. So I know everything is going to be all right." He continued, "If I die tomorrow, because I believe in God, I know I am going to heaven, and I know that one day, you will be there too."

This remarkable human being who never shortchanged others, was seemingly getting short-changed in his life. How could things go so drastically wrong so fast? Joel never felt sorry for himself throughout his entire ordeal. When people visited, they often left without ever asking how Joel was doing. Joel wanted it that way. During this period of gloom and doubt, Joel was always quick to divert attention away from himself and even quicker to direct his interest towards others. He never compromised the high standards he had set for himself at an early age. His highs never got too high, and he never let his lows get too low.

It was decided that Joel had to be airlifted to Johns Hopkins Hospital in Baltimore by medical helicopter. It was hoped that there, some surgeon might have a better understanding of this unusual cancer that was growing throughout Joel's body, and could help him, or buy him some time. With guarded optimism, we were wishing that Joel's race for a long life would be a marathon and not a sprint. Either way, facing life's most difficult problem, it was one more time for Joel to further excel.

Joel had previously informed the Orioles that he was leaving their organization and returning to college. This meant that he was without health insurance. Besides worrying about their son's cancer, financial obligations for his care presented a huge dilemma for the Stephens family. The medical bills were mounting, and continued to rise proportionately throughout the months. Also, there was the added cost of this helicopter flight.

Joel's concern about leaving his family and burdening them with a huge debt was put to rest just before his second operation. Peter Angelos, the much-maligned owner of the Orioles, called Joel frequently to check on his health. During their conversations, Mr. Angelos said that he wanted Joel to receive the best care possible, and that cost should be of no concern. Joel reminded Mr. Angelos that he had left the Orioles a month earlier, and the Orioles were not obligated to pay anything. To the credit of Mr. Angelos, he told Joel he didn't care if he was leaving the Orioles or not. As far as he and the front office were concerned, Joel was a Baltimore Oriole, and he would be treated as such.

Joel was transported to Baltimore, Maryland and placed in the care of Dr. Donehower who is the current Director of the Division of Medical Oncology at Johns Hopkins Hospital. Dr. Donehower worked closely with other current and former star players of the Baltimore Orioles, including Eric Davis, and Boog Powell, both of whom had less threatening forms of colon cancer. Eric Davis was great to Joel while he was in Johns Hopkins. He visited often, and they read the Bible together. Eric even supplied Joel with organic food and drinks, trying to assist in his rehabilitation. It is ironic that Joel was linked to two unrelated men by the name of Davis: Ernie and Eric. The question was which Davis path would Joel follow? Eric survived his bout, while Ernie lost his battle with leukemia.

Chapter 26

Chemotherapy and Treatments

Joel faithfully and devoutly prayed. He was determined to continue to learn, to grow, to become a better person, and to impact lives regardless of the future. He looked at his poor health as a means to become even closer to God. It was November of 1997. Dr. Donehower explained to Joel that this was no ordinary cancer, and that statistically, he had somewhere in the vicinity of three months to live. Because of patient confidentiality, he could not get into specifics about Joel's situation, although he was quoted as saying, "It is not just Joel's physical toughness that impresses me: it is also his mental and spiritual toughness as well. For these reasons, I could never sell this kid short." He also added, "Joel Stephens is one of the most remarkable young men I have ever met. He has had a positive impact on the person I am, and the life I will live from this day forward." Joel wasn't in denial about the seriousness of what was making him ill, and he invested all of his time and energy in trying to get better. He wasn't sitting around and feeling sorry for himself. He understood that this was no ordinary cancer and he wasn't interested in hearing any guesses about how much time he had left. The medical staff fitted Joel with a four-pound mini-pump attached at his waist. This unique device sent chemotherapy directly from a port in his chest to the intestines. It operated twenty-four hours a day, and for as long as Joel could tolerate its strength. Few people would have the grit to withstand the barrage of this potent drug. Dr. Donehower said, "There probably will never be a time when Joel will be off of chemotherapy forever. But he is adding to his quality of life. Nothing he says he wants to do would surprise me." At this time, Joel wanted to recover enough strength to return to baseball for one last at bat. His ultimate dream was to play football at Syracuse before finally venturing into sports broadcasting. Joel was very goal oriented. If he shot an arrow, it was always at some target. His target at this point was to get ready for spring training in the minor leagues and have one last at bat with the Frederick Keys.

Joel spent a few weeks at Johns Hopkins Hospital. In his typical fashion, he befriended many of the doctors and nurses who worked the units throughout the various floors. More important to Joel were the friendships that he developed with the youngsters, fighting for their own lives against a common foe. Joel understood very well the complex nature of their plight. He knew that faith and a positive attitude were essential in battling the disease. He read to the youngsters, their heads bald, bright, and shiny from their treatments. He held their hands and took them on short walks. He talked sports and watched their favorite TV shows with them. He gave them hope. To the best of his ability, he tried to distract their young, innocent minds from their pain and in some instances, their ultimate fate. He was motivating and constructive with each and every one of them, but it was undoubtedly a two-way street. The bonds that were created may have helped to make his own challenge a little easier. One of Joel's most cherished possessions besides his Bible was a white bed sheet that covered him every night. It was unique because of the messages and well wishes his little friends had meticulously scribbled onto its fabric. Joel never allowed it to be washed, fearing that it would damage the gift of their words and their expressions of love. The stories, the posts, the scripture verses, all had a story to tell. Joel left his mark on many at the hospital during that initial stay, and he continued to return to visit his friends and for further consultations with Dr. Donehower and his staff.

Joel walking on his farm during his final days with his chemo pack attached to his hip.

The four and a half hour trip from Tioga to Baltimore for those consultations were bitter sweet. Sometimes the Orioles would provide a roundtrip plane ticket. Other times, Joel would ride in the car with at least one of his parents. Traveling was uncomfortable for him because of the bulky chemo pack and the constant pain. On the positive side, Joel looked forward to talks with his parents, and the opportunity to visit and greet his friends that were still patients at the hospital. When he was too sick to visit other hospital rooms, there was an endless stream of visitors checking in on him.

Chapter 27

Joel Helps a Former Teammate

Life back at our high school was relatively calm, but one day an incident occurred between a student and an administrator. The confrontation escalated to the point where the student kicked out one of the glass entrance doors to the school. I was out of the building at that time but upon my return, I learned that the incident involved a football player who had been in the program since eighth grade. This student / athlete idolized Joel and everything that he stood for. A few years earlier, his parents had divorced and it was not an amicable split. Joel had been playing in his third year of professional baseball and was not aware of the seriousness of the situation and what this teenager was enduring. This student also had some anger issues, and he was taking some powerful prescription drugs to help him cope with stress, depression, and anxiety. Because of this incident and other prior disciplinary referrals, the breaking point had been reached and the student was dismissed from our school. Upon Joel's return from Johns Hopkins Hospital, he was informed about the expulsion. Joel always had a soft spot for this individual and he seemed to bring some stability to his former teammate's life. Joel's sound reasoning and genuine concern always helped to alleviate the worry that bothered his friend. Ralph Waldo Emerson wrote, "The glory of friendship is not the outstretched hand, nor the kindly smile, nor the joy of companionship; it is the spiritual inspiration that comes to one when he discovers that someone else believes in him and is willing to trust him."

I never asked him about his signing bonus with the Orioles, or if he had invested the money where he could claim some big gains. What I do know is that Joel Stephens made investments, and those investments were in his many friends. He was an instant provider of encouragement and support whenever needed. The situation went from bad to worse for this individual. After speaking to him, Joel was very concerned that he might harm himself or someone else. He convinced his buddy that he needed to talk to a professional. Even though Joel was sick and suffering through his own problems, he still managed to visit, talk, and listen to his pal. Joel knew that when we listen and respond effectively, we usually have a greater impact on others. Joel was a great listener and never interrupted others. There were even times when I think he pretended he didn't have a voice. He listened to his friend's cry and he helped. I never understood until later in the year, why this student was reinstated, and returned to his classes at the beginning of the next semester. In a private conversation, Joel had asked our principal if she would do him a favor, and give this person one more chance. Joel knew the importance of a caring community surrounding his friend, and that he wanted to receive his diploma from Notre Dame High School. Joel reminded Sr. Walter that this person needed Notre Dame and Sister agreed to do this for Joel. She did take a big chance, but she had a great deal of confidence in Joel. This story had a happy ending due mainly in part to Joel's concern and goodwill. Given this second life, this student has earned a four-year college degree. He is also raising a family and is currently serving our country as a ranking officer in the military. Joel never got that second chance. Some may say that is because he got it right the first time.

Chapter 28

Joel's Last Winter

The tumor in Joel's colon had grown back and it did not seem as if the chemotherapy was helping to shrink it very much. To eat solid foods was a major chore, and it brought on more pain and discomfort than it was worth. All of his food had to be pureed. This was especially difficult at the Thanksgiving Day festivities in the Stephens home. Despite all the wonderful foods available, Joel was drinking carrot juice. He had lost around twenty pounds, but was trying his hardest to gain some back. Before Lance Armstrong of Tour De France fame made it fashionable, Joel placed a rubber band around his wrist. On occasion, I saw him tug at it. I asked Joel what that was all about. He said, "There are times when I want to eat and I just can't. There are times when I get down, and I don't want to be like that. I just have to snap this rubber band, and it brings me right back and gets my head on straight." I asked him what he had written on it. "Philippians 4:13" was his response. I really didn't know what that scripture verse was, so I waited until I got home to check. It states, "I can do all things through Christ who strengthens me." Joel later gave me his Frederick Keys baseball cap, the last hat he ever wore. On the underside brim of this valued keepsake is Joel's handwritten inscription, "Philippians 4:13."

Joel was still walking the trails and smelling the freshness of the outdoors anytime his body would allow. He continued to lose weight at an alarming rate, and the pain caused him to walk with a bit of a curve in his spine and tipped to one side. One snow-filled winter day, Joel was walking through the woods with his dad and his brother,

Aaron. They were on the boundary of the town's cemetery when Joel gazed up the hill and saw a twelve-point buck, standing perfectly still and observing the terrain. In this cemetery are magnificent headstones, some dating back to the early 1800s. Joel leaned over to his dad and told him that when it was eventually time for him to go to his final resting place, he wanted to be buried where he saw this magnificent deer. These words were very difficult for Ron Stephens to hear but he wanted to remain strong for his son. However, he knew that the time would come when he would have to deal with the last chapter in Joel's life.

That next week, Joel and his mother made the trek back to Baltimore for another treatment. He put on a big façade that he was all right, but the doctors knew that he was in substantial pain. He went through the extensive and painful therapy, took a day or two to recuperate, and then returned home. Late one evening, Joyce Stephens was driving just outside of Harrisburg, Pennsylvania, and Joel with his knees pulled to his chest, was trying to alleviate some sharp pain in his midsection. Somehow, he willed himself to raise his head and in his view through the front windshield, was a large, illuminated cross high on a mountain. Joel asked his mom if she would mind taking him to this place where he could pray for strength and healing. It was around 2:00 a.m. when Joel bowed before the cross. Joel followed the light up the mountain and relied on its conviction. Joel trusted in a supreme being and a higher power. He would soon become the witness and a light for others to follow.

Chapter 29

The Mass

It was early in December of 1997. Joel had been in a fight for his life for almost two months. Nurses visited his home every morning and evening to check on his progress, and to see if they could offer any assistance. Peter Angelos, or someone from the Baltimore Orioles front office, called him on a daily basis to check his progress and to see if there was anything they could do. He continued to receive chemo, drank herbal teas, and took vitamins to overcome his disease. Instead of Joel receiving cheers and standing ovations for his accomplishment in athletics, he now received acclaim for the example he set in trying to beat his new enemy. It was his faith in God, and all the support from his family and friends that kept him focused on beating cancer. He knew that it was his fight, but there were literally thousands that were behind him every step of the way. On December 22, 1997 a liturgy was held at St. Charles of Borromeo Church in Elmira Heights, organized by the diligent efforts of Jean and Cal Keenan. The head of the Diocese of Rochester, Bishop Matthew Clark, was scheduled to say the Mass, but bad weather forced him to cancel his appearance. Father Chris Linsler was the pinch hitter who performed the service. Over the next few months, Father Chris and Joel formed a close friendship. Through the years, I have heard Father use Joel's story in several of his Sunday homilies. A terrible ice storm had marched into our area, causing trees to topple, roads to be impassable, and power outages to occur throughout most of the city. Over five hundred people braved the bad weather and packed the church to capacity. From very young to very old, none let the elements discourage them from showing support and love for Joel. Mary Ann Berrettini, whose son Michael had been a teammate of Joel, made the hour-long trip from Pennsylvania with her family. "Nothing could keep us away from being here. He is a special young man, and he means so much to everyone." I sat with Joel and as usual, he was dealing with some severe pain. Midway through the ceremony, I asked him if he wanted to leave, or at least go to the vestibule in the back of the church where he could lie down. Joel firmly responded, "My friends came out to see me and to offer their support and encouragement. How could I ever even think of deserting them?" I should have known better than to even ask. I had been invited to speak at the Mass by the Keenan family and I said that I would. I do not enjoy standing in front of large crowds, but I agreed because it was for Joel.

Chapter 30

Words to the Church Visitors

I thought long and hard about what I wanted to say. I didn't want to be alarming and paint a picture of gloom. I did want people to understand who Joel was and the seriousness of the situation. I felt that I had to interject some humor in my remarks so that I wouldn't break down. I glanced around the standing room only crowd and knew that a person does not get this kind of respect just because he can carry a football 25 times a game. I proceeded to tell a story of when I saw Joel two days prior, and asked him what he had been doing. He told me, "Reading the Bible, in particular the Psalms." I rattled off, "Listen to me for help," "Hear my prayer," "Do not abandon me," and "Help me to win this battle" when Joel politely asked me how I knew all that. I said, "What do you think I have read before every football game for the last twenty years?" I then turned to Joel to say that it was important for him to understand that:

1. You have many people loving and supporting you.
2. You have touched all of us in a very special way.

Some who were present knew Joel very well. Others knew him only by reputation. Everyone was there to ask our Lord to watch over him, and to bring him to a full and complete recovery. Joel always had great faith, but to the surprise of no one, it had gotten even stronger during this crisis. Facing a grave situation, Joel Stephens again responded in a heroic manner. The true measure of one's greatness is not how they perform in various athletic arenas, but rather how they handle adversity and perform in living their everyday life. In this, Joel truly excelled. We all knew that Joel was an all-star in athletics. What we came to understand was that Joel Stephens was an All-American in life. Here was a young man who never acted like a superstar, nor wanted to be treated as one. In life, when you look at the bigger scheme of things, football and baseball are pretty trivial. Joel's compassion for others, his religious convictions, his humility in his talents, his kindness to all, and his unwavering enthusiasm, all made him what he was. That's what was truly significant and noteworthy. As strong of an individual as he was, he possessed even greater spiritual strength. Even with the catheter penetrating deep into his chest, with constant ripples of chemo being injected into his body, and with all the fatigue and pain it caused, Joel was at peace. Joel believed that his strong convictions in God, many prayers, and the support of his family and friends were essential for him to have a positive outlook, and that they would assist him in defeating this disease.

That evening, the packed church was a true testament as to how one person can affect the hearts of many. This was not for a first down, or even a touchdown. This was a fight for his life, and Joel was well aware of that. When first told of his cancer, he put his father's mind at ease by saying, "Not to worry dad. It's third down and two and I think I can get that." He never thought anything was a problem. Joel Stephens had been dealt a bad hand, but he responded the way everyone knew he would and that was with class and dignity throughout the fight. He knew his opponent and he knew how to push himself. Joel made it through that hour-long ceremony, stood in his place, and briefly addressed the crowd. He thanked everyone and spoke positively of his effort to win his battle. He was appreciative of everyone coming in such terrible weather and said he felt fortunate to be home. When he was finished, the crowd spontaneously gave him a standing ovation. This tribute was for Joel Stephens, the person, not for Joel Stephens, the athlete. Ron Stephens commented, "Even though there hadn't been any organized services to this point, the family and Joel knew that they were getting a lot of prayers and support, and that was important." Brad Polk, Joel's close friend and former teammate remarked, "Joel is treating this just like a bigger football contest. He is going in thinking he will win." Joel stayed at the church for an additional hour, making sure he greeted all of those who had gathered to wish him well. Looking at Joel, many might not have believed he was so ill. Joel, the Stephens family, and I were the only people aware of the incredible pain that he was enduring.

Chapter 31

The Benefit

Nausea and fatigue were side effects of Joel's chemotherapy and it was derailing his workout routine. The container of medicine that was strapped to his hip was limiting his ability to take batting practice at nearby Mansfield University. The only exercise Joel got was walking the fields on his farm and looking for deer. Joel felt that he was getting better, but he looked wiped out and thin to people who hadn't recently seen him.

Everyone who knew Joel wanted to help him in any way they could. A benefit was planned by a number of people in Joel's hometown of Tioga, Pennsylvania, population – 600. This fundraiser was spearheaded by one of Joel's relatives and a lifetime community member, Cheryl Kulago. The spaghetti dinner, sports memorabilia auction, and fundraiser to honor their favorite son was held on January 19, 1998. Although it was organized to raise dollars for defraying mounting medical costs, it was so much more than that. Close to three thousand people attended, and over 2000 spaghetti dinners were served at Williamson High School on that brisk, Saturday afternoon. All wanted to feel a part of that special day and many volunteered their time and services. There were people helping as cooks, waitresses, auctioneers, dishwashers and dish dryers, and everything else imaginable. Many donated a wide array of items including antique furniture, paintings, fresh baked foods, autographed sports items, afghans and oil changes. Someone even donated a vintage 1976 Corvette. The gym bleachers were packed throughout the day, and there was brisk bidding on the raffle items. Many who could not attend sent a monetary donation to the cause. From time to time, I heard the "remember when" stories, when Joel did this or when Joel did that. Joel never truly understood his value to the rest of us. Perhaps this outpouring of love and support in his honor proved to him that so many people held him in such high regard. It is remarkable that this brave man remained so strong and so caring of others, especially after witnessing what he was going through. Those who were close to Joel knew that only good poured from him.

At this time, Joel's weight fluctuated between 170 and 180 pounds but he still had faith. He felt bad that he could not thank each individual personally, but he did find the strength to visit with as many people as possible. Up to this time, Joel had received over 1000 cards and letters. People from the ages of 5 to 75 were writing to him, and he tried to answer every letter. Many viewed him as a role model. A third grade class at one of the Elmira elementary schools studied the story of Joel Stephens, and wrote him heartfelt letters of support. He cherished each and every one. One letter from an eight-year-old meant so much to him that Joel traveled fifty miles to introduce himself to her, and to thank her personally. Michelle Kirby, a forty-eight year old woman from Maryland wrote, "You are the light in the darkness of the world." George Hawke, an inmate at the Elmira Correctional Facility wrote from his cell to me, "I have watched interviews on ESPN and the Empire Sports Network about Joel. With all the bad in the world, and I have seen a lot, I see that there are still plenty of special people like Joel. He epitomizes what is good about people, and especially what is good about our youth." At the end of that six-hour benefit, Joel told everyone, "Seeing all of you and being around so many people means a great deal to me. It is truly amazing and I want all of you to know that I am thankful for your prayers, thoughts, cards, and letters."

Joel and Coach D' Aloisio sharing a lighter moment at his benefit fundraiser.

Chapter 32

Orioles / Others Step to the Plate

Joel could not thank the Baltimore Orioles enough, in particular Peter Angelos. They continued to help with the medical bills. When the Orioles organization learned of the benefit for Joel, they offered the services of Manager Ray Miller, General Manager Pat Gillick, and their number one starting pitcher and perennial all-star, Mike Mussina. These professional and classy celebrities spent hours signing autographs, telling stories, talking about the upcoming season, and doing what they could for their ailing teammate and friend. Cal Ripken donated authenticated bats, balls and a jersey worn by him during a playoff game. Other big leaguers also assisted. Autographed bats and balls came from B.J. Surhoff, Bob Feller, Gary Carter, Kirt Manwaring, Jim Palmer, Jimmy Key, Eddie Murray, Jesse Orosco, Roberto Alomar, and Eric Davis, just to name a few. Buffalo Bills starting quarterback Jim Kelly sent an autographed helmet, and the great running back Jim Brown of the Cleveland Browns, donated a signed football. Other unique sports items included a signed Notre Dame University football helmet and a limited edition, die-cast replica of Dale Earnhardt's race car. Other concerned professional athletes and PGA members Joey Sindelar and Mike Hulbert, both of Horseheads, New York donated numerous items including autographed pictures and golf bags. Mike McCoy, the second overall pick in the 1970 National Football League draft and who had met Joel a few months earlier at a speaking engagement, heard about the auction. From his home in Georgia, he sent numerous signed baseballs of then current Atlanta Braves players including John Smoltz, Greg Maddux, and Denny Neagle. There was even one from comedian Jeff Foxworthy. The memorabilia filled tables and part of the floor that lined the walls of Williamson High School. Mike Mussina signed autographs for hours and had his picture taken with scores of people. The Orioles stood behind their players and this was just another example. Mussina had never met Joel. However, living just a little over an hour away, he knew a great deal about him and what type of person he was. Mike said, "I am proud to finally meet Joel and I am honored to be able to contribute to such a worthy cause."

Pat Gillick was no stranger to the Elmira - Corning area and he still had ties to a few of its residents. The Elmira Pioneers were an Orioles minor league farm team in the 1960s and 1970s, and Pat was an above average pitcher on some of those championship squads. Many at the event recognized him, making him feel even better about what he and the rest of the contingent from Maryland were hoping to accomplish. Pat, along with Ray Miller, talked about how they wanted to begin getting the entire Orioles organization back to being a family. Gillick teared up as he spoke about the rash of bad luck his team was having. Everyone knew that he was referring to Joel, Eric Davis, and Boog Powell, all of whom were battling colon cancer. A few months prior, Mark Belanger, the heralded Orioles shortstop from their World Series championship team of 1983, succumbed to lung cancer, and Cal Ripken, Sr. was not in good health. Pat Gillick remarked, "We believe strongly in putting our actions behind the words. You always hope that something like this doesn't happen to someone who has basically just started his or her life. But Joel never says, 'Why me?' He's so upbeat, so positive. He really thinks he is going to beat this and this type of attitude works in his favor. He's remarkably strong, and he's special."

Mike Mussina bid on a number of items, but he was especially interested in a vintage lithograph of Babe Ruth and Lou Gehrig. Cal Ripken autographed balls sold for $250 each, and his bat and his jersey each went for twice that amount. Two people bought balls signed by Joel for the same price as that paid for those of Cal Ripken. Joel laughed, "I guess they just feel sorry for me." Pat Gillick had to get on the road before the event ended. He approached me to ask what the Corvette was worth. I told him that the appraisal was in the range of $4,500 to $5,000. He then asked me to bid $6,500 for him, and if needed, he would go higher. I don't know if Pat had any real use for this vehicle. I sensed that it would serve as a fond memory of that day, and of Joel, his coaches, his players, and all who stepped to the plate for one of their own. The day exceeded everyone's expectations. It was a small way for many to repay Joel for all that he had given to them. For everyone's thoughtfulness, hard work, kindness, and generosity, the final total raised was well over $30,000.

Chapter 33

The Talk

By February of 1998, Joel had struggled to gain about eight pounds back. Trying hard to keep physically fit, he set his mind on returning to spring training, possibly getting one or more game at bats. Success had never been willed to Joel and he never expected to be handed anything. He continued to work on developing the gifts and talents God had given him, never settling for mediocrity. Joel told me right after he was drafted, that if he ever did make it to the big leagues, he would take care of Jayne and me. That was very unselfish of Joel, but I told him that it was his work ethic that got him to be a professional player, not other people. I told him that he didn't owe anyone anything. He strongly disagreed with me. I then said, "Oh! By the way, could you autograph these half-dozen baseballs that I just happened to have in my desk?" He sat down and began signing. Knowing that I had just pulled one over on him, he looked at me and had this big smirk on his face.

Joel was regularly invited to talk at banquets and ceremonies anytime his health would permit. Many times, he was not really up to it, but he had this problem of saying "No" to anyone. Invariably, he entertained the audience without complaining.

One afternoon, he stopped at the house and asked if I wanted to go to lunch. I ate while Joel picked at his food. We went for a ride and came to a stop at the top of Harris Hill. This is one of the highest points in Chemung County where people can look down and see the valley in all directions. Our discussion was turning sentimental when

Joel asked about a story I used in one of my talks. I recalled hearing
it at a homily given by the deceased Fr. Chris Gramhke, pastor of St.
John's Parish in Elmira. The story goes like this: "A man was given a
tour of both Heaven and Hell so that he could intelligently select his
final destination. The Devil was given first chance to impress the man
so he started his 'prospect' with a tour of Hell. The first glance was
surprising because all of the occupants were seated at a banquet table
loaded with every food imaginable, including meat from every corner
of the globe, fruits and vegetables and every delicacy known to man.
The Devil pointed out that no one could ask for more. When the man
looked carefully at the people, he did not find a single smile. There
was no music or indication of gaiety generally associated with such a
feast. The people at the table looked dull and listless and were literally
skin and bones. The man noticed that each person had a fork strapped
to their left arm and a knife strapped to their right arm. Each utensil
had a four-foot handle that made it impossible to eat. So, with food of
every kind at their fingertips, they were starving.

"The next stop was heaven where the man saw a scene identical
in every respect – same foods, knives, and forks with those four-foot
handles. However, the inhabitants of heaven were laughing, singing,
and having a great time. They were well-fed and in excellent health.
The man was puzzled for a moment. He wondered how conditions
could be so similar and yet produce such different results. The people
in Hell were starving and miserable, while the people in Heaven were
well fed and happy. Then he saw the answer. Each person in Hell had
been trying to feed himself. A knife and a fork with four-foot handles
made this impossible. Each person in Heaven was feeding the one
across the table from him."

This was one of Joel's favorite stories. I realized that this was a
story about Joel's life, about his actions, and how quick he was to help
others. I told him that he was the person feeding others, especially at
this time in his life. He cared for others, and he always valued them as

individuals. I asked him soberly, "Joel, what do you think is going to happen?" He said, "Deep down, I think I am going to be OK. Either way, I know that I have tried to live my life like I think God would want me to. If I have helped one person on this planet, then I would say that I have been successful at what I wanted to accomplish." I then asked him if he was afraid of dying. "I don't really think about it, but no," was his reply.

Some may say that life is not about the destination, but rather about the journey. To Joel, the destination was just as important because he already knew he would be in heaven someday. That was his ultimate goal. However, the journey was equally important because it laid the groundwork for his entrance into Paradise. To countless others who followed and understood Joel's journey, it helped make them become better fathers, mothers, brothers, sisters, and friends.

After that, I looked to the blue sky where a few puffy white clouds had gathered. I asked Joel what he saw. He said that the clouds looked to be an angel, or Christ with arms that were gloriously spread. Amazingly, I had the same vision of what was hovering high over our heads.

Chapter 34

Acts of Kindness

Joel had been given 3 months to live in November of 1997. Four months had passed and his last CAT scan didn't show any change in the tumor. Joel had beaten some stiff odds other times in his life, but there was a big difference this time. One of the times he may have cheated death was immediately following his last season of baseball. On his way to Hawaii, he and some fellow players stopped in Colorado for two days to do some white water rafting. Joel told me that he had never been more scared in his life. The raft had tipped and he and another passenger got stuck among the rocks and branches deep beneath the water's surface. Just about out of breath, Joel used every ounce of his strength, pulled free from the debris, and got to his buddy. In a matter of seconds, Joel tugged his friend from the rubble and they both made it back to shore. Joel had dodged one bullet, but could he do it again? The time frame of ninety days to survive his disease had passed, but I wondered again and again, just how much tread was left on Joel's tires. I tried my best to get it out of my mind, but I couldn't abandon this negative thinking.

After the benefit and many newspapers articles on Joel, the stream of letters, cards, and gifts resumed in full force. Even Michael Jordan of the Chicago Bulls had somehow heard about Joel because he sent him an autographed basketball and his best wishes.

Joel always appreciated everyone's thoughtfulness. One moment that was truly memorable and inspiring to me involved Joel and eight-year-old, Patrick Sullivan. Walking up to Joel, Patrick was carrying an autographed basketball that looked very familiar to Joel. The young boy had recognizable features but at first, Joel couldn't recall the lad's name. Then he knew. Joel took himself back approximately four years to when he was playing in the Crusader Classic Basketball Tournament. This was the same young boy who had been fighting his own cancer. This was also the same ball that Joel had presented to then five-year-old Patrick Sullivan after winning the tournament's Most Valuable Player Award. With a tone that was barely audible, Patrick told Joel that he was now cancer free, and he thought Joel would have better use for that ball this time. I have never heard Joel speak when every word rolling off his tongue was difficult to express. To say he was touched would be a gross understatement.

Joel attended New Covenant Church in Mansfield, Pennsylvania. It seemed as if everyone in a hundred mile radius was following the saga of Joel Stephens. I would venture to guess that the church's congregation might have increased due to Joel's influence. While a parishioner, Joel met a nice family that was struggling with relationships and financial issues. One day, Joel called my office and asked if I was going to be around. He said there was an eighth grader that he wanted me to meet if I had the time. I always had time, or would make time for Joel. Forty-five minutes later, he introduced me to Luke Whiteker. Joel had taken Luke and his younger brother, Nick, under his wing. Nick was battling juvenile diabetes and Luke, solidly built with blonde hair, resembled a smaller version of Joel. Joel wanted Luke to attend Notre Dame High School in September, but his family did not have the finances to pay the tuition. Joel became Luke's mentor for the next six months, helping him out with life lessons, as well as financially.

Of the $32,000 that had been raised at the benefit, Joel kept only a small portion. Just before the fundraiser, Joel had met an eight-year-old boy who was battling Non-Hodgkin's lymphoma. The boy's name was Eric Schall and Joel became friends with the entire Schall family. They obviously were worried for their son and there were times when the Schall's felt overwhelmed. Joel's easy and confident demeanor helped the family put their trust in the Lord. Dave Schall, Michele Schall, and the children (Mike, Matt, Christine, and Eric) were a solid, loving, caring, and altruistic family. Joel often said that the Lord does not give anyone anything they can't handle. Joel helped the Schall's deal with this setback by showing great faith and confidence that Eric would be all right. He visited Eric almost daily and I'm sure he made a substantial contribution to his little friend's hospital bill. What was most important to Eric besides a clean bill of health was that Joel promised him two things. First, he was going to get him a Baltimore Orioles jacket. Second, he promised to take him to the Little League World Series in Williamsport, Pennsylvania that August. Dave Schall wrote to me, "Joel continues to fulfill his mission to help others, and all should be proud of him. When people share a common direction, and a sense of community, you can always get where you are going more quickly. That is because you travel on the trust of God, and one another. We have drawn from Joel's strength and encouragement, and we will never give up." Eleven years later, Eric is cancer free, and like his brothers, is a very good athlete.

Talk is cheap, but vision is true. It was February of 1998 and as concerned as I was about Joel's health, I was confident that he would keep his promise to Eric. A promise from Joel was as important to him as food, sleep, water, and oxygen.

Chapter 35

Making a Difference

The nurturing of the bamboo tree should serve as an example for all of us to follow. It is clear that Joel's early years parallel the development of a bamboo tree. The moral fiber and good habits that were instilled in Joel came from his strong family background. They were the basis of a solid foundation in the formation of Joel the person.

For many in the world, the bamboo tree is a natural resource and serves as a food to nourish and sustain life. When its seed is first planted, it must be continually watched, watered, fertilized, and tended. It needs sunlight, nutrients, and climate conditions that are ideal in order to achieve successful growth.

On the surface, the bamboo plant grows very little during the first 3 to 4 years. What the naked eye can't see is the sophisticated and intricate root system that is being developed beneath the surface. There cannot be any shortcuts in this process. During the first years, the tree needs to get established and may only reach a few feet in height. However, somewhere in the fifth year, during a 6 to 8 week span, the plant grows to almost full maturity, reaching approximately 90 to 100 feet.

Joel's life paralleled the bamboo tree. His strengths were solidly rooted in faith, hard work, enthusiasm, and respect for others.

Life has to have challenges for people to reach their full potential. Without adversity, there can be no miracle. Joel welcomed all obstacles and despite insurmountable odds, Joel continued battling his more-than-formidable rival. He believed that tough times had value because they provided a way of getting closer to God. Tough times don't last, but mentally tough people do. Physically, Joel was getting weaker, but spiritually he grew stronger each day. He often quoted a passage from the Apostle Paul, "So that now as always, Christ will be exalted in my body, whether by life or death. For to me, to live is Christ and to die is gain." He knew that his body was letting him down but ironically, he felt bearing this burden and serving as an example for others was easier that hitting a 90 mile per hour fastball. A devout Christian, this had been God's plan and it was Joel's belief and faith in this plan that drove him forward. Joel and his mom talked frequently about his ability to influence others. In these conversations, Joel revealed that he had been talking to the Lord, and that he would do what needed to be done when it came to helping others. That was his primary goal in life. Major league baseball was important, but his disease was the greater avenue in extending himself to others. A goal without action is called dreaming. Action without a goal might be considered wasting time. A goal with action is making a difference and changing the world. Joel's vision to make a difference and change the world occurred long before he became terminally ill.

A few months before Joel's sickness, he had become friends with a man named Charles S. Alsheimer. This name may not be recognizable to many, but to hunting and photography fans, he is legendary. For close to forty years, he has been prominent in these fields, and he is the author of a number of books as well. His work has appeared in numerous outdoors and wilderness publications. Charlie and Joel were strong Christians, and it was natural for those two to inspire and teach one another, even if for only a short time. Joel accompanied Charlie on several hunting and speaking engagements in the next few months. They discussed at great length God's impact on life and how they wanted to continue to grow in their faith. Charlie wrote that Joel had a tremendous impact on his life in the short time that he had known him. "He truly was sent from God to touch people's lives." Joel also thought a great deal of Charlie and his passion for nature and for God.

Joel was always very comfortable in the woods. A tree, a frozen pond, a bird, a flowing brook – the simplest pleasures always left an indelible mark on him. He took it all in as if he were a sponge.

In the spring of 1998, three generations of Baltimore Orioles afflicted with colon cancer were asked to throw out the ceremonial first pitch at an exhibition game. This game took place at Camden Yards versus the New York Mets. Former first baseman Boog Powell, then current center fielder Eric Davis, and minor league outfielder, Joel Stephens were making this 'Pitch for Prevention' to emphasize the need of getting regular physical checkups. Joel and his girlfriend, Erin Wood, watched the game from the box seats before they returned home that evening.

On May 15, 1998 Joel was the honored guest at the fourth running of the Tioga County Cancer Relay for Life held at Mansfield University. It also happened to be his twenty-second birthday. This relay is a 24-hour event that runs from Friday evening at 4:00 p.m. to Saturday evening. The committee had asked their local celebrity to be their honorary chairperson. Money raised from this relay was used to help cancer patients in the Mansfield / Tioga areas with medical costs, treatments, transportation to therapy, etc., as well as to make a donation to the National Cancer Society. Joel and many family members pitched tents, brought sleeping bags, food, supplies, and other necessities, committing to the cause, and partaking in the festivities for the entire 24 hour duration. Joel was on hand to talk and visit with fans and participants, both day and night. He was not satisfied until he had put his own fingerprints on the event. While walking his scheduled hour shifts, Joel occasionally broke into a light jog. Always feeling that he could do more, Joel organized a softball tournament that ran concurrently with the relay. This allowed people who were not scheduled to run, to have a few laughs and play for some balls and bats that Joel had donated from his playing days.

I know that Joel kept thinking about his possible return to Maryland, and taking a game swing with the Frederick Keys minor league baseball team. Before that, however, Joel still had work that needed to be completed closer to home.

Betsy Tokarz, the co-chair with Joel, wrote four months after Joel's death, "When I think of Joel, certain words come to my mind: God, faith, family, love, commitment, encourager, strength, and honor. I worked with Joel on the Relay for Life Committee, and he was an inspiration to me, and to the entire committee.

At the time he and we all thought he had the battle won and he was helping other people with their battles. He was tired because he was still taking heavy treatments, but he gave everything he had to make the event a huge success. Joel had certain abilities that made him very, very special. Some were athletic, but the dominant one was his love for the Lord and his family. Joel was always a testimony to anyone he met and he always wanted to share the Good News about his Lord. Joel has been taken from us at a very young age but the way in which the Lord used him in these short years will more than likely put the rest of us to shame in our longer lifetimes. We say that Joel has lost the battle but I think he is really the winner because of the way God used him while he was here. I know in our hearts and minds, Joel will always be a part of the Relay for Life. Thank you, Joel Stephens, for the many things you taught all of us."

Cheryl Clark, editor of *Tioga Connections* and in charge of public relations for the Tioga Relay For Life told people that Joel meant so many things to so many different people. He had been asked to help and he did the only thing he knew how to do and that was to totally commit to this endeavor. Dangerously exhausted and fatigued, Joel was the major reason why the "Walk" exceeded everyone's expectations, and generated $20,000. That was double the amount that they had raised the previous year. Cheryl remarked, "Joel has literally laid down his life to be of service to others." She recommended that all future

Tioga County Relays for Life be named "The Joel Stephens Memorial Relay For Life."

In early June of 1998, Joel was having his good days and his bad days. He was asked to say a few words at the Dave Smith Cancer Walk in Sayre, Pennsylvania. It turned out to be one of those bad days, but he would never turn away anyone's request for help. I knew Joel was very weak. I asked him what they expected him to do and he told me that he was supposed to be at the stadium around 3:00 p.m. I offered him a lift and he accepted. He was supposed to speak to the teams and participants about the value and purpose of these walks, culminating with him starting the event. One hour, two hours, three hours passed, and Joel still had not given the introductory speech. The organizers had a change of plans and felt that it would have more of an impact if Joel spoke prior to the luminary service. This would be the most opportune time to honor those present who were living with cancer, and the families and friends who had lost loved ones. Joel wasn't scheduled to speak until sometime between 9:30 p.m. and 10:30 p.m. I mentioned to Joel that this wasn't the initial plan, and that he needed to get home and rest. I offered to tell the committee and knew that they would understand. Joel refused to leave. I was upset because Joel needed sleep, but it didn't seem to bother him. We sat at an uncomfortable picnic table while Joel chatted with the large crowd that had gathered around. He felt it would be disloyal to the organizers if he left. He needed to stay so he could accomplish what they had asked of him. He asked me not say anything about any inconvenience and that he was doing fine.

Although he was too sick to be there on that day, Joel was called to the press box around 11:00 p.m. and spoke from the heart. He had stayed over eight hours when he should have been out of there in thirty minutes. Standing at Joel's side, I glanced over the stadium bleachers where hundreds had taken seats. There was not one dry eye in the place as those in attendance focused on Joel's every word. "Please, don't feel sorry for me," he said. "If you want to feel bad for anyone, give your help and prayers to the little kids and the other 600,000 people in the world who die every year from cancer." My special friend had once again made it through a difficult day. In beating the odds, if only temporarily, he captivated all of us with his will to survive and his ability to keep up the good fight.

The Smith family appreciated Joel's presence. Joan Smith commented after meeting Joel and hearing him speak, "He is a very courageous young man. I will always remember him for his kindness, and for his faith in the Lord, Jesus Christ. I am especially honored and privileged in knowing him."

Chapter 36

Television Interviews

Joel was the favorite of the sports media for obvious reasons. He was talented, photogenic, intelligent, and interesting. Always candid and articulate, he spoke from the heart and generally refrained from giving the standard answer. Joel granted interviews to many local newspapers and radio / television stations from Baltimore, Maryland to Rochester, New York. The major sports networks did features on Joel including ESPN and the Fox Sports Network, and the Associated Press also ran a story on him.

Josh Mora, a Florida native, was a popular sports television personality working in our area when Joel was playing high school sports. He was very talented and people knew he was destined for a better job in a bigger market. I hadn't heard from Josh in over three years, when out of the blue, he gave me a call. He had recently taken a position in Buffalo, New York working for the Empire Sports Network. Josh had followed Joel's career and now wanted to interview him as his first assignment. I arranged for Josh and Joel to meet at Notre Dame High School the next day at the baseball game. This was during the first week of June in 1998. Josh was eager to do this story and he was even more excited about visiting and sharing stories with Joel. Josh conducted the interview seated outside of the leftfield foul line. They talked for over an hour. The show aired on television a week later. Josh did an outstanding job of sharing Joel with his viewers. He prefaced the interview by saying that this was one of the greatest stories in Elmira sports history and that Joel was fighting his biggest battle yet. The similarities between Joel and Ernie Davis were again discussed. Watching this program, it was clear that these two similar gentlemen were also gentle men. Josh remarked that sometimes you meet an athlete that changes the way you look at sports. Then there are the truly great athletes who have an even greater impact, making you think about your life and everything else that's important in the world. For Josh, Joel Stephens had that type of impact. Josh continued, "Joel Stephens is an affirmation of everything that is good about people, and about sports."

Josh wanted to talk about the gravity of Joel's medical situation but Joel refused to dwell on it. Joel briefly commented that even though he was receiving chemo twenty-four hours a day and had not eaten anything solid for the last 7 or 8 days, he felt great. Joel went on, "I am glad I have this illness. I feel I can be an example and a witness to my faith for others to follow in tough times." When Josh asked Joel if he considered himself a role model, he quickly talked about others who were motivating him, especially eight-year-old Eric Shall who was battling his own cancer. He was Joel's role model. With all the talent in the world, Joel displayed a deep modesty and never felt he should be put on a pedestal. To him, the role models and heroes were the teachers who brought knowledge and inspired the imaginations of young children. Heroes were the doctors and nurses who brought comfort and happiness to him and to others. People who volunteered at the soup kitchens and who sheltered the homeless needed to be recognized, not him.

Peter Angelos had made Joel a priority and Joel was proud to be a part of the Orioles organization. Even though he wasn't a major leaguer, it was gratifying to know that people thought of him that way. Joel told the viewing audience that he had put all of his faith in the Lord, and that the Lord would provide. He still wanted to travel to Frederick, Maryland for the exhibition baseball season, and to have one official at bat with the Keys. When posed the question, "Would that be your definition of a perfect ending?" Joel replied, "That's my definition of a great beginning."

Homerun king and Hall Of Famer Henry Aaron said at his induction ceremony in Cooperstown, New York in 1982 that "The way to fame is like the way to heaven." People have to persevere through difficult times in order to attain certain goals. Henry Aaron had to deal with racism and jealousy. Joel Stephens had to deal with a terminal illness. A crisis can characterize an individual's mettle and exemplify one's beliefs and values. Joel, like Henry Aaron, affected thousands, many of whom neither man had ever met. When tragedy strikes, it is widely felt. Joel Stephens saw his illness as a blessing, not a curse. Joel stood proud, he stood tall, he smiled, and he never quit. Unlike Henry Aaron, Joel never made it into the baseball Hall of Fame. However, through all of his trials and tribulations, he used his people talents and all the abilities that God had given him. He developed his character to the best of his ability and for that he was awarded a greater induction. That took place just three short months after the Josh Mora interview, and it was Joel's Hall of Fame induction into heaven.

Chapter 37

One Last at Bat – Joel's Kids

After Joel's interview, I had to leave while he stayed and watched the game and chatted with friends. His car was still at my house and he hitched a ride with Mike Tobin. Mike was a childhood buddy in his late forties, an avid sports fan, and known by almost every high school athlete and coach throughout New York and Pennsylvania. For close to thirty years, he seldom missed an athletic contest. Nicknamed "Tobes," he used to be a hellion. In 1970, coming home from his correctional officer's job near New York City, he crashed his red Dodge Charger and instantaneously became a paraplegic. Even though paralyzed from the waist down, Tobes remained tough, living alone and remaining independent. Confined to a wheelchair, Tobes always seemed to have health issues after the accident. A rejected kidney transplant left him needing dialysis three times a week. It wasn't uncommon for Tobes to know all the athletes through the years and he considered Joel the best. He also regarded him as a good friend. Tobes' black Legend van pulled to our house and Joel stepped out. Jayne saw them arrive and invited them in for dinner. Joel helped Tobes with the process of moving him from the car seat to the wheelchair and to the lift, and then of transporting him up the steps to the house. We ate dinner and Tobes was again off to watch a night softball game. Joel reversed his earlier actions, getting Tobes back in his van so he could be on his way.

Once the van left, we sat on the front porch with Joel wanting to know more of what happened to Mike Tobin. I told him that Tobes had lost his parents early in life. He had a difficult childhood and it was reflected in his poor attitude. Some people said that Tobes might have been lucky to be paralyzed because if he wasn't, someone may have killed him a long time ago. Whether true or not, Tobes was a survivor and his deformed arms and lifeless legs were visible proof of his resiliency and durability. Joel thought for a moment and said, "Dialysis has to take a lot out of Mike." I agreed that it wasn't easy for him and that he was exhausted after every treatment. Joel told me that he wanted to find out if he were a match so that he could donate a kidney to Mike Tobin. During the interview that day, I know that Joel told Josh Mora he was doing great. Those close to him knew otherwise. He had lost fifty pounds and he looked very gaunt. His skin had a grayish hue and his eyes had sunken deeper into their sockets. Just three years earlier, an Atlanta Braves scout had said that Joel was as strong an eighteen-year-old as he had ever seen. I tried to be diplomatic and mentioned to Joel that his near term goal was to get that professional at bat and not to cheat himself of the opportunity. He had worked hard trying to strengthen his body and he was only two weeks from returning to the Frederick Keys in Maryland. I had taped Joel's television interviews and when I played them back, I noticed an accelerated decline in Joel's physical appearance from one show to the next. I let him know that wanting to donate a kidney was a generous gesture and it was a very special act when someone is willing to give the gift of life, but for now he needed to put that thought on hold.

To me, and to others, Joel was looking worse. In my heart, I felt that the cancer had invaded Joel's entire body and I was pretty confident that no organ was free of its grip. A week after Joel's death, I told Tobes what Joel wanted to do for him. Mike Tobin was truly touched and for the first time in my life, I saw this tough man break down and cry.

Even though cancer weakened his body, Joel's mind was still strong and sharp. He volunteered to help Harry Hilson run a summer baseball camp for boys 8 to 12 years of age. Harry is the highly successful head baseball coach at Mansfield University. Joel felt that he would get as much out of the camp as he would give. Just to be around young people and baseball seemed therapeutic for him. Somehow, possibly through a greater force, Joel willed himself to temporarily rally.

Joel's original plan was to attend the Oriole's rehabilitation camp in Sarasota, Florida and then report to the class A Frederick Keys by the end of July. A month earlier, CAT scans revealed a pretty clear picture with spots previously seen on the liver now gone. Doctors at Johns Hopkins could not explain it and Joel told them that it was the power of the Lord. His fortitude and faith were second to none. The doctors didn't disagree.

Joel skipped Florida and went to Maryland, intent on giving everything he had to make the Frederick Keys baseball team. He didn't want preferential treatment, nor did he want people feeling sorry for him. If he couldn't make the squad on his own merits, then he didn't want to be a burden to the coaches or a detriment to the team. Miraculously, Joel participated in every drill and sprint. As frail as he was, he still found time to volunteer his services at various events in the community. After one week, Joel became very sick and returned to Johns Hopkins. The spots on the liver had returned. He also had to deal with a serious blood infection and with an obstruction in the intestines. All were praying in Frederick that he could make an appearance on the very last day, but he was just not feeling up to it. Before Joel departed the Frederick Keys clubhouse for what turned out to be the final time, he left a haunting note hanging on the wall. "To everyone, best of luck this week. I have to go home for a week and return to Johns Hopkins for a couple of tests. Don't worry though. The Lord is taking care of me. Take care and God Bless – Joel."

However, throughout the previous week with the Keys, he touched everyone in a very special way. One person in particular was Mark Zeigler. Mark was the Public Relations Director for the Frederick Keys. Joel had such a positive impact on Mark that after hearing of Joel's death, Mark established the Joel Andrew Stephens Memorial Hospice

Foundation, a.k.a. "Joel's Kids" in 1999. The Joel's Kids Foundation has mainly benefited youth groups and non-profit organizations in Frederick County, Maryland, as well as aiding individual youngsters who are dealing with adversity / handicaps, and / or a bereavement due to the death of a parent, grandparent, or sibling. Mark's goal was to keep the legacy of Joel Stephens alive. He said, "Joel's unselfish behavior, strength, and courage to help those less fortunate were among his special characteristics which are the basis for this charity named in his memory. Through 'Joel's Kids,' the spirit of Joel Stephens will live so that the youth of Frederick County can receive the one more at bat that he was unable to achieve." To date, the Joel's Kids Foundation has given thousands of dollars to such Frederick County organizations as Challenger Little League, Thorpe Wood, Inc. Family Support, Andrew J. Jones Windows To The World Sheriff's Youth Boys Ranch, and the Frederick County ARC.

Chapter 38

Dedication of the 1998 Football Season

I have been coaching for over thirty years, and I have never asked any of my teams to dedicate a game or season to any individual or cause. The right to victory belongs to those who participate and to all who have invested their own time and sweat into determining the final outcome. 1998 was the exception. The players and coaches decided to keep one of our finest alumni and greatest former players in their thoughts and prayers, and to honor him in how they played, and how they conducted themselves throughout that football season. The person who received this unusual honor was a humble, unassuming high school icon and role model named Joel Stephens.

As a constant reminder of our pledge, the coaches and players conceived the idea of wearing three-inch, orange sweat bands with a navy blue number 24 tackle-twilled and stitched into its fabric. The navy blue represented our high school's dominant uniform color, the school that Joel represented and honored so well. The number 24 was the number worn in high school by Joel and retired by the school's football program upon his graduation in 1995. The orange signified three things. In 1994, Joel signed a letter of intent to attend Clemson University on a football and baseball scholarship. After doing some serious soul searching, he dismissed this opportunity, instead opting to sign a six-figure major league baseball contract with the Baltimore Orioles. Joel spent three years in the Orioles organization as a power-hitting outfielder, but his inner desire was to play football at the Division I level. He was offered a full scholarship to play football for

Syracuse University. The one constant in all three of these organizations (Clemson University, Baltimore Orioles, and Syracuse University) is that the dominant team or school color is orange. This band worn by the coaches and players served as our special way of acknowledging someone whom we respected. Many fans followed suit, wearing ¼ x 2" blue and orange strands of ribbon that were attached to an angel charm, showing their support as well.

The second way the team wanted to pay tribute to Joel was that each player wore a gold sticker the size of a silver dollar bearing his initials (JS) on their blue helmet. Our school colors are blue and gold. These two gestures by the team were to let Joel know how important he was to us and that we were keeping him in our thoughts and prayers.

Football double sessions began in August of 1998. Joel helped at practice whenever he was available and feeling well. With only five starters returning, the newspapers did not paint a rosy picture for a successful season.

Our season opener was scheduled at the Carrier Dome in Syracuse, New York on Sunday, September 6, 1998 against a solid program from Sauquoit Valley High School. This "Kickoff Classic" had schools from Elmira competing in games all afternoon against teams from the Syracuse area. Joel rode the team bus and moved from seat to seat, mingling with the players and coaches. Instead of just traveling with our team, Joel should have been suiting up for his own college games on the same field. One way, or another, Joel had made it to the Carrier Dome sidelines. Quarterback Mike Meck had almost completely recovered from a gunshot wound to his chest, and he needed to be our field general for us to succeed. However, it was Joel Stephens who served as our off-the-field inspirational and spiritual leader.

In the locker room just prior to taking the field, the coaches went over our 'Keys for Success.' I gave my final reminders to the team and then asked Joel to say a few words. He talked about how football was such a great game, and we always needed to see the big picture, whether in sports or in life. But most of all he said we needed to go and have fun. He finished with the comment that "Success is that peace of mind one gets in knowing that they have done their best, and we should do it that way all the time. Stay focused, stay positive, and let's bow our heads and say the Hail Mary." Joel led us in prayer and finished it with our traditional invocation, "Our Lady, Queen of Victory," to which everyone responded, "Pray for us."

The game was a rout and could have easily been even more lopsided. We played well but we still made mistakes. First game jitters may have come from the awe of playing for the first time in the Carrier Dome, and from wanting to play so hard for the man to whom we had dedicated our season. As the final horn sounded, a number of our players shook Joel's hand and told him to look at the scoreboard. The final score was 24-0. It just happened to be his jersey number and the number we were wearing on our wristbands.

Chapter 39

Joel Travels to the West Coast

The team won its next two football games but Joel was losing his individual battle as his health continued to decline. Running out of options, Joel decided to travel to Mexico for experimental cancer treatments to extend his life. His parents and his pastor, Rod Murray, supported his decision and accompanied him on this journey. The doctors in Mexico began treating Joel, but nothing seemed to work. Kevin Malone, General Manager of the Los Angeles Dodgers, lived not too far away from where Joel was staying. He and Joel had developed a solid friendship when Kevin was Assistant General Manager of the Baltimore Orioles. He visited Joel regularly while Joel was on the West Coast. Kevin, Pastor Rod, his parents, the doctors, and the hospital support personnel, all tried to make Joel comfortable. The cancer had now invaded his spinal column and he was in excruciating pain. Joyce Stephens called me at school on Thursday, September 17, 1998. They had run out of options and she was looking for help. I suggested that they transport Joel from Mexico and have him admitted to a hospital in the United States. It was important that they get him home where he could be in familiar surroundings for the last days of his life. I would only have to make one phone call to get the help we needed.

I decided to contact Bob Agan. Bob was a self-made man who worked his way through the ranks to become the Chief Executive Officer of Hardinge, Inc. Hardinge is a large company that manufactures machines and has clientele worldwide. He had also been the president of the Board of Governors of Notre Dame High School.

Bob offered his help to many whenever possible, but he always tried to keep his involvement quiet. Regardless of his attempts at anonymity, his kindness and benevolence throughout our community was well known.

I shared with him my conversation with Joyce Stephens a few moments earlier, and made it clear that Joel was dying. We needed to bring him back home to his family and friends as soon as possible. I asked him for the services of his company's jet. Bob said he would make some phone calls and get back to me. Within ten minutes, Bob called and said that Doug Tifft was in his office, and I could speak to him to work out the details of the flight. Doug was a friend from our basketball playing days, and Director of Personnel for Hardinge. He told me that the plane and the pilots were ready to go on a moment's notice, and added that he wanted to accompany me on the flight to San Diego, if I didn't mind. The jet seated eight passengers and was just large enough to bring us back, but we would need to put the luggage in another plane due to weight restrictions.

I called Joyce Stephens and told her that the plane was ready. She said that the doctors performed a spinal tap on Joel to relieve pressure on his brain, and that he was now resting comfortably in his room. A conference with the oncology staff was scheduled for Friday, September 18th. After this meeting, all would be ready to return home early Saturday morning. I contacted Doug Tifft and we made plans to leave Elmira on Friday at 2:00 p.m. I still couldn't believe that we were given the company jet with no questions asked. My wife suggested that it might be wise to bring along a nurse, just in case something happened to Joel while in flight. She asked Joan Genzel, a registered nurse from St. Joseph's Hospital in Elmira if she was available to do us a favor. Without any hesitation, Joan agreed to give up her weekend plans, especially for a patient she had admired from a distance working at the hospital over the last ten months. Joel's reputation continued to be a positive influence and served as an example, bringing out the very best in others. But then again, many knew Joel would have done the same for them.

One small problem before we left had to be addressed. The football team was playing and I was going to miss the game. Before I left school on Friday, I called the team down to the locker room to tell them of my plans. The coaches and players agreed that it was more important to bring Joel home than it was for me to be at the game. I told the team that we had had a good week of practice and that they would do fine. The captains hugged me one by one and made sure that I told Joel that this contest against Groton, our undefeated opponent, was for him. As I boarded the plane, I noticed that the two pilots appeared to be younger than Joel and they sensed my nervousness. I prayed for a smooth flight, but more importantly, I prayed for a peaceful return trip home with Joel.

Chapter 40

Touch Down

We made stops in Detroit, Michigan and Pueblo, Colorado before finally touching down at the San Diego airport around 9:00 p.m., PST. During the flight, Joan and Doug read while I just stared out the window, wondering how Joel was feeling. After the plane landed, Ron Stephens met us at the gate with a van ready to take Joan and Doug to the motel and me to the hospital. As we were leaving the airport, an employee approached our group and asked if one of us was Ron Stephens, or Coach D'Aloisio. Ron had a look of concern on his face. Any unsolicited call during this time was likely unwelcome. On this occasion, however, it was a bit of good news. Someone from the school had called the airport and left a message, Notre Dame Crusaders – 34, Groton Indians – 0.

As we entered the hospital, a doctor and two nurses greeted us and asked if I was Joel's former high school coach. I said that I was. They felt that he was a pretty special person, and then proceeded to tell me what had happened a day earlier. They mentioned that Joel was in horrific pain while Mexican Customs stopped the hospital's vehicle. The Mexican border police were checking cars when they came upon the van. These policemen, the U.S. hospital attendants, the Stephens family, and Pastor Rod Murray watched as the pain intensified. All expected Joel to say, "Please help me Lord." Instead he broke his silence saying, "Lord Jesus, I thank you and praise you for this suffering. I know you suffered for me and I feel your pain. And I love You Lord Jesus, with all my heart, and with my mind, and I will

accept this suffering. It doesn't matter to me. I will always love you."
Still conveying his message, Joel thanked the Lord for allowing him to
be His witness. He bowed his head and folded his arms, took a deep
sigh, and proceeded to pray silently to himself. The customs officials
were deeply touched and felt they were in the presence of someone very
special. They blessed themselves and allowed the medical van to bypass
fifty cars and continue on its way.

At the hospital, I came around the corner into Joel's room while he
was talking to Kevin Malone, former Assistant General Manager of the
Baltimore Orioles and now the General Manager of the Los Angeles
Dodgers. Joel looked up at me and said, "Oh my God! I don't believe
it! Coach D, what are you doing here? Don't we have a game tonight?"
I said, "We've already won. I'm here to get you back to the farm for
some good home cooking." He jumped up and we hugged. Joel's
frame was so thin, a far cry from the muscle-layered body he had just a
short time back. He introduced me to Kevin and asked if I wanted to
go for a walk around the hallways. We were excited to see each other.
He gave me a surge of energy and I feel that I gave the same to him. We
walked, we talked, and we laughed. Hearing his voice was consoling
to me, even if momentarily giving me a false sense of hope. I told Joel
that we were leaving at 6:00 a.m. and he needed to get some rest. I met
him at the airport on Saturday, September 19th. The ambulance arrived
and Joel climbed out of the back seat. He asked me if I would mind
doing something for him. I asked what before I agreed to it. "Would
you mind jogging to the plane with me?" I mentioned that at my age
that might be a problem, but that I would do my best. As we started, I
glanced at Ron Stephens. He didn't want his son to see him get choked
up, so he turned away as Joel and I trotted down the runway.

Once we were in the air, Joel, whose seat was opposite mine, became
sick to his stomach, and the altitude didn't seem to be helping. He tried
to eat some Danish pastries and I think that was for my benefit. The
plane had to land a few times, hoping to alleviate the pressure in Joel's

head. I stared at Joel and he at me. He didn't have to say it but Joel knew that he wasn't going to be with us much longer. Unfortunately, he knew that I understood this as well.

I called Jayne the night before to say that I had arrived safely, and asked her to have an ambulance at the Elmira airport for Joel upon his arrival. No one was supposed to know that Joel was returning home. When we landed at the Elmira – Corning Regional Airport around 2:00 p.m., there were over 100 people gathered outside of the terminal. Joel was too weak to walk off the plane without assistance, but he would not allow that to happen. As the ambulance crew began to walk up to get him, he appeared in the plane's doorway and came down the steps. The crowd saw him and began to cheer. Joel and I lagged behind the others who were on the plane. We had our arms draped over each other's shoulders. Just before Joel was to greet the crowd, he leaned into my ear and said, "Coach D, keep your dreams big and your worries small, and certainly don't worry about me. I am going to a better place. Thank you for getting me home, but now I am tired, and I am ready to 'Go Home'." We broke out of our embrace with Joel heading towards the crowd, and me heading towards Jayne. I couldn't stop crying, telling my wife what had just happened. I added, "Joel's work on earth is just about done. We are not going to see someone like him ever again."

After the plane's arrival in Elmira, the ambulance that had waited for him would make the additional forty-five minute trek, returning the Stephens family to their farm in Tioga, Pennsylvania. The end was drawing near, the final storm was close, but he was not afraid. Joel understood a rainbow would soon appear, and he would be free of the intense pain that he had had to endure for over a year. Once home, he would be nestled safely in the environment where he was raised, sensing the comfort, contentment, and solitude that the familiar sounds of the outdoors and the beauty of the surroundings would bring to his remaining days.

As Joel's coach and friend for the past eight years, I requested that the family keep me updated in his unrelenting and dogged determination to fight for his life. The colon cancer that had wreaked havoc on his body for the past ten months now had a firm hold and was ready to deliver its final and decisive blow. It would tear down and disable his body, but it could never touch his spirit, nor diminish his faith.

Chapter 41

Joel Inspires N.D. Win

It was Saturday, September 26th and somehow, Joel found the strength to ask his father to bring him to his alma mater's high school football game in Tioga, New York, which was close to a two-hour journey from their home in Tioga, Pennsylvania. Knowing how sick his son was, Ron Stephens reluctantly agreed to help his ailing son into their Jeep. It was a beautiful day and he thought that the fresh fall air might just do some good for both of them.

The undefeated, state ranked Notre Dame Crusader football team was in a real dogfight, a scoreless tussle with an old nemesis, the Tioga Tigers, when the horn sounded ending the first half. Oblivious to everything that was going on outside of the white lines of the football field, my attention was more focused on stopping our opposition and winning the second half. It seemed that everyone except me noticed that Joel and his dad had obtained special permission to drive their vehicle onto the field of "Jim Haggerty" Tiger Stadium. Here they could watch the remainder of this daytime slugfest with a bird's eye view from the corner of the northern end zone. As the second quarter was ticking away, Joel asked his dad if he could get him bottled water from the concession stand. Ron Stephens knew that this was just a ploy used by Joel to get him away from the vehicle so that Joel could attempt to leave his wheelchair and visit our sideline without any assistance. Once his dad was out of the general vicinity, Joel, although weak and frail, managed to walk the sixty yards to meet with the team that he had been following and motivating since September. This feat seemed pale in comparison for someone who only a few months earlier ran the length of a football field, or rounded the bases with the ease and silkiness of DaVinci's brush painting the Mona Lisa. As the teams took to the field preparing for the second half, I was the only person at the game who didn't realize Joel was there. Eventually, I recognized a familiar voice from behind me on our sideline, speaking to our quarterback, Mike Meck. A week earlier, the players had been informed that Joel had taken a turn for the worse, and they were astonished to see him standing with us on this day, proud of the team that he had adopted as his own. To my surprise, Joel was emphatically suggesting to Mike that "Coach D" was getting worried, and his blood pressure was rising like the shuttle going into orbit. Joel urged Mike on by adding, "Let's get this machine in gear and start playing this game to win it."

Mike Meck knew what Joel meant to everyone, but he especially knew what he meant to him. Three weeks before that start of the football season, Mike had been shot in the chest and his non-throwing arm in a hunting accident. Mike miraculously recovered, partly due to his own toughness, partly due to the help, prodding, and support of Joel. Mike took Joel's sideline statements and advice on that day as gospel and proceeded to reduce the coaching staff's stress levels, reeling off touchdown runs of 77 and 83 yards on the first two possessions of the third stanza. We played a perfect second half. A reporter asked Mike what it meant to have Joel with us. Mike responded, "Anything that Joel says, we all listen to and take very seriously. I told the team that Joel is on our arms, he is on our helmets, and he is on our sidelines. What we are playing for is him and let's not let him down." Jake Fiamingo, our all-state linebacker said, "Just to see him at our game made everyone step it up a notch. Just think how many notches he had to step it up just to be here." Sometimes, the smallest gestures have the greatest impact. Even though Joel was emaciated and gaunt, his face sunken and drawn, he was still inspiring and willing us to win football games, and we did not want to let him down. Final score: Notre Dame 14, Tioga 0.

After the game, the team presented Joel with the game ball. It was the last ball he would ever carry.

Chapter 42

His Shrine

On the Stephens farm, deep in the woods and nestled among the beautiful birch and pine trees sits a shrine where Joel prayed and meditated daily. At this improvised altar hangs a homemade oak cross. Surrounding the altar, trees have been cleared with their stumps serving as nature's pews for all visitors. On each side of the cross rests a wall of stone serving as candleholders, displaying their blackened ash stain from daily use. With the sounds of geese overhead, or an animal rustling the leaves close by, or maybe no sound at all, here Joel was content and at peace.

This outdoor temple served as a safe haven where Joel had conversations with the Lord. Its tranquility lifted his spirits. He tried to understand his fate and what his "Master Teacher" wanted him to do. He asked what his role should be throughout his ordeal. He prayed for others and he prayed for strength. He prayed for the ability to remain strong in commitment and character. Reputation did not mean a great deal to Joel, but character was always at the top of the list. I recall showing Joel a quote by John Wooden, saying that you should be more concerned about your character than your reputation. Your reputation is how others perceive you, but your character is who you really are. Joel asked me if I thought he was a good person. I replied, "My God, you have to be kidding!" He had an impeccable character. He was raised to do the right thing, and his legacy would survive because of who he was. So soft-spoken, so humble, so giving and caring for others, he almost was too good to be true. I felt that he was a treasure that needed to be shared.

When Joel was near death, the Stephens family, as well as the Elmira *Star-Gazette* asked me if I would write something about Joel that could be used as a press release. I grabbed a pencil and paper and visited the shrine that Joel and his dad had built a few years earlier. I asked the Lord for help so that I could do justice to Joel with my words. I was writing a eulogy for one of my closest and dearest friends and I was scared.

Joel was spiritual, he practiced gratitude, he nurtured relationships, and he always worked hard at keeping himself physically fit. He had reached the pinnacle of his athletic career for all of his hard work. He had blessed us with everything good. It was time now for him to reach the top of his spiritual world. I tried to think of ways that Joel wanted to be remembered. I flashed back in my mind and recalled a story of George Brett when he retired. Brett was an infielder for the Kansas City Royals, and one of the best baseball players of all time. As his career was winding down, a reporter asked him how he wanted his last play to go, and how people should remember him. Many would want to hit a walk off homerun. Others might want to hit a grand slam in the bottom of the ninth on a 3 and 2 count and with two outs to win a World Series. What George Brett said astonished the reporter. He hoped to hit a soft, lazy two-hop grounder to the second baseman. After contact, he sprints out of the batter's box and hustles as hard as he can to beat the throw. The second baseman fields the ball cleanly, makes the throw to first base, and Brett is called out just before he reaches the bag. He wanted people to know that no matter what, he hustled and gave everything he had to play the game correctly, right to the end. I wanted people to understand that Joel played the game of life the way it should be played, and he did it that way until his last breath. He gave it his best. He gave others his best. He kept trying and he never quit. His entire life was the best game he ever played.

Chapter 43

Excerpts from Guest Column

On Wednesday, October 1st, the Elmira *Star-Gazette* published an article I wrote to honor Joel in the "Guest Columnist" section of the newspaper. The following are some excerpts from that article as well as other lines from my notes:

Joel Stephens' courageous and final battle has ended. This man was as unique and rare as the cancer that took his life.

There are times in everyone's journey through life when we reflect on someone who has touched us so deeply and in such extraordinary ways. This is not a story about how this "awesome" man died, but rather about how he lived.

It is hard for me to fully comprehend that on those hot, muggy, and buggy summer afternoons, and coming off a tough football game, Joel patiently found time to talk to everyone. He uncomplainingly signed autographs, or posed with a picture seeker, never looking perturbed or annoyed. He found time for everyone. It is impossible to describe the looks of joy on the faces of those fans. What a sharp contrast it is in this present day, when many star athletes are in it to make a quick buck adding to their astronomical salaries and charging huge fees for autograph sessions. More than his athletic talents, it was his inner qualities that really won the hearts of others. Treating others well and with respect never had an off season with Joel. Joel would never have the opportunity to get to the big stage where he could sign a multi-year, multi-million dollar contract. I am convinced it would not have changed him at all. As gifted as he was as a player, he was even more gifted as a person.

When I think of Joel, my mind is instantly flooded with a thousand electrical currents, each one carrying a special memory of our fallen hero. Yes, I said "hero" because that was Joel Stephens. This is not a term that I casually toss around. Even though Joel did not ask for this title, and was humbled by its label, he had earned it. Hero is not a title bestowed on someone because he scored X-number of touchdowns, or hit Y-number of homeruns. Rather, this term is used to signify excellence of character, and the courage to be different. Joel Stephens was different, and God certainly knew that Joel Stephens was special. People feel helpless when they don't know what to do during a crisis. For twenty-two short years, Joel knew exactly what needed to be done. He gave two of the world's most precious commodities to countless others: himself and his time.

While out in San Diego and suffering unbelievable pain, Joel raised his hands to the heavens and thanked the Lord for choosing him to be the one to bear the pain so no one else would have to endure his agony and suffering.

Joel once again responded with dignity and class, serving as an inspiration to countless thousands from coast to coast. His resolve, fortitude, and influence gained momentum as his illness grew more and more severe. Nurses, doctors, friends, and outsiders all whispered in amazement at his physical and spiritual strength. They also openly marveled at this person who seemed larger than life, having that same life cut all too short, eventually succumbing to a rare and dreaded form of colon cancer.

Joel Stephens was a miracle and it was in what he gave to others that he truly excelled. Yes, he was an all-star in athletics. But to those who witnessed his love, he was an All-American in life. He was that star who never acted like one nor wanted to be treated as such.

Joel's unique capacity to touch and influence others, regardless of race or religion, has been rivaled by only a few. He was a man of few words, but his actions spoke volumes.

For example, in his last weeks on earth, although unable to eat solid food for days, he kept his promise by taking an 8-year-old cancer patient to the Little League World Series in Williamsport, Pennsylvania. To Joel, a promise was a promise, and a commitment was a commitment. Loyalty to him was as important as oxygen, food, sleep, and water.

He was devoted to his family, his friends, his teammates, his coaches, and to his fellow man on the street. But above all, he was always true to his faith.

I'm sure we all remember his brilliant play on the fields. It did not take long to realize that Joel Stephens was not just another "face in the crowd." His talent and skill, driven by a dedication to excellence, his outstanding sportsmanship and his intense desire to win and never give up, cried out with an eloquence that could not help but be recognized by his fellow players, the press, coaches, and all who loved him. He was this, but he was also so much more. He was not your typical high school star whose glory was going to fade on graduation day.

To be honest, Joel Stephens was the closest thing to a son I had. I will think of him often, and he will help motivate me to become a better teacher, coach, and more importantly, a better person. His untimely death has left an emptiness in many of us that refuses to be filled. We will miss Joel and his absence will leave an ache that can never be soothed. In our minds, we will continue to see him smile. In our hearts, we will recall with warmth and affection, his wit, his kindness, his generosity, and his giving and open nature. We remember him – what he was, what he said, what he accomplished in his short time with us, and we cannot help but be moved and inspired by these memories.

Joel never questioned his faith or his religion, many times publicly stating that he was happy that he was burdened with his affliction. He used his illness as a platform to reach out to more people, never seeking to be rewarded but never quite content or satisfied in what he could give to others.

We who carry on realize that during our lives we were privileged to have been touched by an angel, someone who was truly great, an example of the best that humanity can become.

155

Joel made me look good as a coach, but he made me a much better person by watching how he lived his life. Because of life lessons that Joel taught, I owe him a debt that can never be repaid.

It has been said that God visits this garden he calls earth every day. He often picks the biggest and the brightest of all his flowers. On September 30th, He picked Joel and decided to take him home. As much heartache that many have felt through Joel's ordeal, I would not want to trade one second of it. He was someone you felt fortunate if you had the opportunity to meet once in your life. God blessed many of us in our area because we had the great opportunity to be touched and influenced by Joel Stephens.

Joel Stephens was a good person long before he was stricken with the disease that ultimately claimed his life. He felt the Lord chose him to illustrate his greatest battle and toughest test, the test of one's faith. Having maturity beyond his years, he understood that victories don't just come on the fields and the courts. He realized that it was his illness that would create an even larger forum for him to set an example of his belief in a higher power. After he found out he had cancer, Joel commented, "I feel that this is a blessing in disguise. Without cancer, I could have never reached out to as many people that I've been able to reach out to now." Joel knew that beating cancer was a miracle that was not likely to happen. Whether Joel died today, or in one hundred times one hundred days, he knew where he was going. His final destination would be heaven. To him, that was the ultimate change of address, and he lived his life to become a permanent resident. He would accept it when it happened. But until he took his last breath, his battle was waged. After his diagnosis, he was even more committed to show others that as a Christian, he continued to assume the role of a God-fearing, living example of one's faith.

From this moment on when you talk to me, I will tell you about Joel's touchdown runs and about his hits. More importantly and with tears filling my eyes, I will tell you about my friend and his life story. That is the reason that I decided to write this book. The story of Joel Stephens had to be told.

Do I believe what has transpired? Frankly, no, but I will accept it because Joel would want it that way. Jayne and I feel we have lost our heart and our soul.

Like Joel, I also believe that someday we will go to a better place and be together once again. That's why we will go on. I prayed for a miracle, but now I realize that the miracle was the Lord loaning us Joel and having him with us at all. He left us better people for knowing him. He left us wanting more. We will cherish those memories we have of Joel Stephens, and we will not let his life go unnoticed. That's because those same memories will keep him forever close to us.

So now the Lord's team is complete. Let Joel round third, carry the ball, run to 'home' and fulfill his last championship. Let him achieve his greatest victory and let heaven be the prize. Guide us, watch over us, and pray for us. And until we meet again my friend, Jayne and Coach D. will always love you.

Chapter 44

Safe at Home – Joel's Final Hours

Divine intervention was not to be. In a time of blemished stars, winners with ego problems, and athletes with skeletons in their closet, Joel personified decency and righteousness. During his final days, Joel said to his mother, "If this is all God has given me, then that is what I have and I can accept it, and I loved and cherished every minute."

He left us on September 30, 1998 in the "Joel Stephen's Way" with dignity and class.

On Sunday, September 28, 1998, Joel had fallen into a coma. Family and friends kept a round-the-clock vigil at his bedside. People prayed, touched and rubbed his hands and head. They gave him sponge baths, sang his praises, and cried. At one point, Joel summoned his strength, opened his eyes, and gazed to the heavens in a dream-like trance. His eyes sparkled and were animated as he stretched his hand skyward and held up his index finger signaling number one. A peacefulness and calmness came over him. Then returning his hand to his chest, he lightly pounded his heart three times. He did this four to five times. Several people witnessed this and questioned what it all meant. They asked, "Is he saying he is number one?" The people who asked did not know Joel as well I did. There were many times that people told Joel that he was great, or he was awesome. I would hear the same response roll from his mouth. "I am not great, and I am not awesome. The Lord's awesome and great. He is number one, and He is in all our hearts." I like to think that Joel saw Christ calling him, and that he was extending his hand to go with Him.

Jayne and I spent over thirty hours at the Stephens home and we needed to get home to check on our parents who were also ill. Jayne was very concerned that Joel would die after we left, and she wasn't so sure that that would be a bad thing for me. She knew this would be traumatic for everyone and especially for me. We discussed this on our drive home. I felt that Joel would survive until we returned in a few hours, and I told her that I was prepared to deal with his death. When we returned to the house, it was approximately 8:30 a.m. Most were sleeping or sitting in the kitchen, just waiting for the inevitable. Joel was meticulous about his appearance and other than being very thin, looked as if he was relaxing in a power nap. He was draped in the white sheet with scripture verses and well wishes that the sick children from Johns Hopkins had written to him. While we knelt at his side, my wife, Joyce and Aaron Stephens washed Joel's face and hair, as I feebly attempted to encourage him that it was OK to let go. "For one last time, take that mighty swing and make contact with the ball. As the ball finds the gap, you round second base and head for third. The relay is perfect, setting up for a close play at the plate. The on deck batter is frantically signaling you to slide to beat the tag. The catcher cleanly fields the throw, but your honest effort allows you to be safe at home. Your reward is not the scored run, nor is it another six points for a touchdown. Your prize is much, much greater. This time, your reward is peace and eternal life in the presence of our Lord in heaven." Seeing a tear trickle from the corner of his closed eye, I knew that he heard my words. Joel continued to fade over the next hour with his mom and dad closest to and hugging their son. This outpouring of love and affection was almost overwhelming. Jason Chapel, Joel's best friend since second grade and who was in the room on this day later said, "Some people only know Joel for his sports. I have been so lucky to have him as my friend. He was always there for anything I ever needed. I can't imagine my life without him." Joyce, Ron, and all other family members offered assurance that heaven was waiting for their newest angel. Perhaps it was maternal instinct, but Joyce Stephens knew the precise second that her son left his body. She asked the nurse to come closer and take Joel's pulse. Her intuition was correct and Joel had taken his last breath.

When he died, we coped with his death the only way we could, and that was to take one day at a time. We knew many would never get over him, but we hoped our heartache would lessen as the days passed. It is in giving that one receives, and no one gave more of himself than Joel. There was a solace in knowing that he was finally pain free. More importantly, we realized how lucky we had been to know Joel, and how fortunate we were to have been touched by his love. His light showed the way. It shone most brightly when there was darkness and despair. People felt he could move mountains, and I thought that one of the world's super heroes had died. A slogan in a popular TV commercial suggested, "Life is short. Play hard." In Joel's case, it was shockingly short. Joel deserved a better fate.

Chapter 45

A Good Person

Engraved on Joel's gravestone located in Evergreen Cemetery in Tioga, Pennsylvania is a passage from the Bible Verse, Philippians, Chapter 1:19-21. It reads: "For I know that through your prayers and the help given by the Spirit of Jesus Christ, what has happened to me will turn out for my deliverance. I eagerly expect and hope that I will in no way be ashamed, but will have sufficient courage so that now as always Christ will be exalted in my body, whether by life or death. For to me, to live is Christ and to die is gain."

Joel's gravestone at Evergreen Cemetery located in Tioga, Pennsylvania.

Many were in a state of shock after hearing of Joel's death. They prepared to pay their respects to someone who offered them a multitude of life lessons. Joel had done so much for people's faith that they felt the need to give something back. Assistant Principal at Notre Dame High School, Sr. Nancy Kelly said, "Joel never doubted that God had a plan for him. Many people looked up to him and I think that he would want those same people to live on with the same strength, courage, and faith that he had."

It was Friday, October 2, 1998 and the parking lots and streets in downtown Mansfield, Pennsylvania were filled to capacity. An estimated 4,500 to 5,000 people attended Joel's wake held at the New Covenant Parish Center. When I entered the hall, it almost seemed as if the walls were crying. Roped off aisles resembled a maze that mapped the course for visitors to follow, allowing them to move along in an organized pattern. This took 2 to 3 hours, eventually leading them past a display of Joel's memorabilia and ending with the Stephens family. Just a few steps away, Joel lay in his casket, surrounded by a garden of flowers of all colors. Here people could say their individual prayers for and to their special friend. Shortly before Joel succumbed to cancer, he had a talk with his mom and dad. He asked that at his wake they display his Ernie Davis Award and none of his other trophies or jerseys. His parents asked why. Joel replied, "The other awards are nice and I know I worked hard to earn them. However, I won them because God gave me some decent talent. The Ernie Davis Award is special because it meant that I was a good person, and that is how I want to be remembered." The family rightfully overrode Joel's request, displaying items along with his Ernie Davis trophy on this sad day. It was a special honor for Jayne and me because we were asked to stand with the family as they greeted people. Joel's body was close enough for me to look down and see his serene face. This was a far cry from a week prior when this same face expressed so much pain. Lying in the casket, he was wearing a light blue oxford shirt and tie and a handmade tan sweater vest. This is what he wore on special occasions, and sometimes when he spoke at banquets. It made him look even more rugged than he already was. The Scureman Funeral Home planned well in advance, realizing the difficulty of accommodating the crowd that would be coming to see Joel. They also did a great job in presenting Joel to his fans, making him look as if he was resting and still healthy. Bill Thomas, the former Corning East baseball coach said as he knelt down to pray at Joel's side, "When I look back at our championships, I will recall there are more important things in life. I am thankful I coached baseball because I was able to cross paths with Joel Stephens. He simply was the best." The showing was scheduled from 2:00 p.m. to 7:00 p.m. but it went closer to midnight because of the steady stream of people that kept filing into the makeshift funeral parlor. Notre Dame High School's assistant football coach and a friend of Joel, Jeff Sobkowski, said, "If you were ever wondering if grown men cry, let me tell you that after today, they do." Another assistant coach, John Mirando, remarked, "Joel is one of those kids that come along once in a lifetime. His story is one that movies are made of." Ron Stephens said, "Joel is home free. He has the No. 1 coach now and he is proud of it."

Joel had no regrets. He had no ill feelings. Rather, he had thankfulness that he had the pleasure and opportunity by the grace of God to make some very good friends and have some very fond memories along his journey.

The Stephens family never sat down nor did they ever leave the greeting line. Thinking like their son, they felt that if people were kind enough to visit, they had to be there for them. There were many touching moments, but there is one that was truly memorable. A young boy came through the line and approached the family. I saw him wearing a little Baltimore Orioles coat. When I asked him if that was his favorite team, he said it was. I then asked him where he got that sharp jacket. He told me that Joel had bought it for him. At the moment when Ron introduced me to the child's family, I realized that this was Eric Shall. This was the same little eight-year-old boy with Non-Hodgkin's Lymphoma whom Joel had helped a few months earlier. It was around 1:00 a.m. when Ron and Joyce left their son and returned home to try to get some rest. They knew that with the funeral scheduled for the next morning, things were not going to get easier for them.

Chapter 46

Joel's Funeral

Our next game was to be played out of town on Saturday against Newark Valley. They moved the game time from 1:30 p.m. to 11:00 a.m. in order to accommodate people who wanted to attend Joel's funeral. Jayne and I left the game midway through the second quarter so that we could be at the church. A victory was well in hand but it didn't matter. There wasn't any way that we were going to miss the service. We won that game 34 to 22.

Once the game ended, everyone was looking forward to returning home for next week's homecoming game after starting the season with five consecutive road games. But first, we needed to pay our respects to Joel at his funeral.

Joel's absence from our world made many feel empty. Over 600 people attended the funeral held at the Church of the New Covenant which doubles as a recreation hall in Mansfield, Pennsylvania. On the front door of the sanctuary was the number 24 Notre Dame football jersey that was worn by Joel during his high school career. His number 27 Delmarva Shorebirds baseball jersey hung on another door inside the entrance way. Along with these jerseys was the Bible Verse, Psalm 37:23, which reads: "The steps of a righteous man are ordered by the Lord." Many attendees to the funeral wore Joel Stephens' buttons with his picture on them, or memorial ribbons that his elementary school used as a fundraiser. Joel lay in an open casket at the front of the altar where the surrounding bleachers were covered with a shrine of floral arrangements and photographs.

"Joel was such a tremendous young man as an athlete, a tremendous human being and a tremendous member of our society," said Corning West High School coach Lou Condon. "He was the example that we asked all of our kids to follow and he was an all around wonderful person."

Lou's counterpart at Corning East High School, Randy Holden, commented, "After spending some time with Joel, I could see how the whole community was enamored with him. He was the type of kid you prayed to God that your own kid would grow up to be like."

Pastor Rod Murray started off the service by setting the record straight. "We are not here to be sad, but rather to celebrate a life in Christ." Pastor Murray lightened the mood with some humor. He mentioned that he and Joel often sang religious songs to raise his spirits while he was in the hospital. Pastor Murray continued, "It is safe to say that Joel was a great athlete. It is also probably safe to say he wasn't an entertainer," referring to Joel's singing voice. He continued to say that Joel's last wish to us was that his parents, family, and friends be with him in heaven someday. The Pastor then opened the altar to anyone who wanted to share thoughts of Joel.

Among those in attendance were Pat Gillick, General Manager of the Baltimore Orioles, and Syd Thrift, Director of Player Development for the Baltimore Orioles. Gillick said, "On behalf of the Baltimore Orioles and myself, I would like to extend my condolences to the Stephens family. It has been an honor getting to know Joel. He was a very unique and special young man, one that I considered my friend and admired a great deal. His faith and courage were a lesson for all of us. I only wish that more people could have experienced Joel, because they surely would have been touched by his life the way we were."

Terry Mickey, an elder at the church, said that Joel had an influence even on people that never met him. "That's the kind of outreach he had. Without a doubt, the people he's met will always remember him."

Dr. Donehower, Joel's oncologist from Johns Hopkins, echoed the same sentiments. Upon hearing of Joel's death, he said, "Joel was blessed with great talent, but never had a chance to achieve a full measure of success – and that's what makes it profoundly sad. Joel Stephens' story touched the lives of many who never met him." The doctor elaborated, "Fully one-third of my own patients have asked about Joel. Somewhere, I think, he realized that what he was going through, at his age, struck at the basic chords of humanity. And he talked about it. I'll never forget him. I'll remember details of my conversations with Joel, and what it was like to know him for the rest of my life."

Mike Isenberg, a sports commentator from Elmira who then was working for ESPN Sports, approached the microphone to say a few words. Mike and Joel knew each other very well and became close after numerous interviews that Mike had conducted. Mike drove through the night to Tioga from Springfield, Massachusetts where he had been covering Larry Bird's induction into the Basketball Hall of Fame the night before. When speaking to the crowd, Mike referred to a quote from Martin Luther King, Jr. "The ultimate measure of a man is not where he stands in moments of comfort and convenience, but where he stands at times of challenge and controversy." It is easy for people to be brave when all is going well for them and when they are prospering. It is how Joel stood tall in the face of tragedy that truly separated him from others. Mike felt that Joel showed tremendous courage when he was presented terrible odds. Now, Mike felt a duty to show courage and speak on this day, knowing that it would be difficult to deliver his talk without breaking down.

Ted Bowers, a close cousin of Joel, spoke and asked everyone to stand and give an ovation for Joel. "We owe him that," he said. People were used to cheering for Joel's athletic exploits. Now they rose and applauded him for over three minutes for his accomplishments as a person.

Fr. Chris Linsler who officiated at the Mass for Joel in December wished to add another line to Joel's obituary. "Add major leaguer, because Joel is now in the major leagues."

Joel embraced his sickness and carried his cross with joy. Joel wanted people to take a look at their own life and figure out ways to make others feel good. Even though his need to get healthy was great, he preferred to pray for others. One of Joel's last comments was read at the podium. "In a lifetime, one will face many tests of faith. How you deal with these tests makes you the person you are. You can't control what is going to happen to you, but you can control the faith you have in the One who has complete control – our Lord Jesus Christ."

Chapter 47

Helping Others

I was too shaken to speak but Pastor Murray did read some lines from my remarks that I had previously prepared for the Elmira *Star-Gazette*. In the car on the drive back to meet with the team and the coaches, I mentioned to Jayne, and to John and Carol Layton (Jayne's brother-in-law and sister), that someday, something will happen and I am going to say, "That was Joel." John asked, "Like what?" I replied, "I don't know. Something like we are going to win the lottery, or someone is going to live that should have died, or someone is going to miraculously recover from an illness. It will be something that when it occurs, we are going know that Joel is watching over us." It wouldn't take long for this to happen. Even though Joel's voice has been silenced, I feel that he is forever with us.

It was the Monday after Joel's funeral around 5:00 p.m. and I had to stop at the grocery store. I picked up a dollar Win Four straight-box lottery ticket with Joel's football and baseball numbers on it (2427). Later that evening, Jayne and I were watching television and the winning numbers for that day scrolled across the bottom of the screen. As they came by for the second time, I told Jayne that we had just won $2,750. Jayne watched as the numbers came in straight, 2-4-2-7. We looked at each other and said, "It's Joel." We decided that the Notre Dame football team needed new jerseys and we purchased new uniforms for the football team in Joel's name.

During the first week of December in 1998, my two nephews, Dan and Joe Bennett, and their friend, Pat Mustico, were traveling to Pat's house at 2:00 a.m. All three were former athletes at Notre Dame who were home for the weekend from college. Dan was on a baseball scholarship to William and Mary. Joe was attending Wyoming Seminary Prep School on a football scholarship, and Pat was a student at St. Bonaventure University. All of them looked up to Joel as their role model, especially Dan who was a teammate of Joel's in football, basketball, and baseball. Joe Bennett was driving, and on a dark, country road, they hit a patch of black ice and slammed head-on into a tree. The three boys crawled unscathed from the wreck and proceeded to walk two miles up the road to my parent's house. There they called the state troopers to report the accident and then met them at the scene. I got a call from my sister letting me know what happened, that the car was totaled, and that the boys were pretty rattled. I went to the accident scene as quickly as I could. As people approached the scene, no one could figure out how anyone could have survived that crash. The troopers shined their flashlights into the front seat and onto the floor of the car that now looked like an accordion with wheels. Face-up, underneath the steering wheel was a framed collage of Joel Stephens. Joe Bennett had made this to hang on his wall at school when Joel died. This picture collection had been missing since October and Joe couldn't remember where he had placed it. The impact of the accident was so forceful that it dislodged it from underneath the driver's seat and it was now there for all to see. Joe then realized where he had put the frame. The three boys felt that Joel was still watching and caring for them. Glancing back at the car, they were my sentiments as well.

Chapter 48

Football without Joel

Usually, great teams are that way because they form a bond by going through adversity together. The 1998 Crusader football team had been through a great deal but they never lost focus on Joel to whom they had dedicated their season. They continued on their quest for a state title.

On September 30th, the day Joel passed away, I called our principal from the Stephens' farm and relayed the information. Sr. Mary Walter made an announcement to the faculty and students over the school's intercom shortly thereafter, and there was a school-wide moment of silence. Counselors were made available in the library if students needed to speak to a professional about their emotions. Around seventy-five students took advantage of this service. I returned to the high school at 3:30 p.m. to meet with the football team and to begin practice. I was a few minutes late and the assistant coaches had already begun the stretching drills. About ten minutes earlier, the area was soaked with a torrential thunderstorm. Then the sun began to shine brightly as steam was rising from the pavement and off of the cars in the parking lots. I called the team over to give them a firsthand account of the earlier announcement. Joel had died and I explained how his strength and unwavering faith carried him to his last breath. I told them that the world was a much sadder place with the loss of our friend. The Lord just got the first pick in the football draft and our loss would be heaven's gain. The players were huddled and on one knee when members of the media began approaching our circle. They felt our pain and understood our sorrow and honored my request of not granting any interviews at this time. I mentioned that the photographers were welcomed to take pictures and to film drills if they wished. As I continued to speak to the players, I wanted them to understand that Joel wanted us to advance on our mission, and that we still had plenty of work to do. Joel accomplished what he wanted in his short 22 years on earth. It was our turn to attain what we had set out to do. As I was wrapping up the events of the past few hours of Joel's mortal life, our big tackle Matt Hammond said, "Hey, look at the stadium field!" As all heads turned away from the practice field and stared towards the stadium, we saw that a rainbow had formed from the prior storm, and it was covering one of our end zones. The players and even the coaches felt that the Lord was giving us signs through Joel that everything was going to be OK. How strange it was to have this majestic array of colors hovering over our field when this entire day had seemed so dismal.

It was Friday, October 9, 1998 and there was a huge crowd for our homecoming game vs. the Lansing Bobcats. Paul Titus, our junior varsity coach and the announcer for the home varsity games, asked everyone before the opening kickoff to bow their heads and say a prayer in memory of Joel. After this, Paul directed the fans to look at the flagpole located at the scoreboard end of the stadium. On one side of the American flag was a pole that carried a flag commemorating the U.S. soldiers who had given their lives in service to our country. On the other side and waving from a newly installed pole on our scoreboard was a banner that read, "Number 24 – Forever In Our Hearts." From this day forward, this gold and blue flag honoring Joel has been displayed at all home football games.

The Crusaders beat Lansing, then Watkins Glen, and were undefeated heading into our last home contest against a high scoring outfit from Trumansburg. Prior to the start of football, expectations were not running very high for achieving a solid season with that year's team. The coaching staff felt the players had not put in the time during the off season that typically proved to be our recipe for success. However, Joel changed all of that. The players worked very hard to make amends for their lack of effort in the summer. Through Joel's example, the players felt that they could accomplish anything. On this evening, the proud squad of Trumansburg had the faithful fans of Notre Dame nervous, leading 16-14 as the halftime horn sounded. After making some halftime adjustments, we scored the first two touchdowns of the second half, but Trumansburg continued to hang tough. With less than thirty seconds left in the game, and Notre Dame finally in control of this 50 to 30 offensive shootout, Ryan Ollock intercepted a pass by Trumansburg in their last-ditch effort for a win. As I watched the interception, out of the corner of my eye, I noticed a shadow coming in my direction. I jumped back thinking that someone had thrown something. I quickly glanced down our sidelines and saw assistant coaches Dick Craft and Brian Sheehan jump out of the way, and on down the line as players imitated our move. I asked, "What the heck was that?" The players and coaches told me that a white bird, or pigeon, had darted through the members of our team. It was close to 10:00 p.m. and many fans sitting in the stands saw this strange occurrence. Dan Zeller, our defensive end and the school's valedictorian that year, said it looked like a white dove. People believed that it was Joel once again making an appearance and exhibiting his approval. There are too many coincidences for me to say otherwise.

Chapter 49

Joel's Inspiration

Our last two home games of the season were played on cool and clear fall nights. Normally, there are thousands of stars in the sky. During these games there was only one. We had lost Joel and we were hoping that his shining star was watching over us. Our eight-game regular season had ended without a loss. In our first post-season game, we were paired against Unatego at Ty Cobb Stadium in Endicott, New York. We were quickly down 14 to 0 when I called a time out to help calm our nerves. Just before play resumed, our center, Chris Bennett, noticed that a very large cross high atop the hill and opposite our sideline was now radiantly glowing in the moonlight. He mentioned it to his teammates on the field and the game quickly changed in our favor. We scored the next 38 points. Scott Grenolds returned an interception for a touchdown and Dave Noonan and Mike Meck each rushed for over 140 yards to secure a 38-14 victory. As our bus was returning home, the players pointed out the cross to the coaches. They also noted that the color of the large, neon cross just happened to be orange. Maybe our players just had vivid imaginations, but I have gone from a skeptic to a sincere believer.

The next game for the sectional title was against perennial favorite, the Walton Warriors. As we arrived at Cornell University's Schoellkoph Field, I was greeted by retired New York high school coaching legend, Fran Angeline. Coach Angeline offered me his condolences about Joel and asked, "Was he the young boy you mentioned for me to watch back years ago when he was a freshman?" I commented, "Yes he was, but now we hope he is watching us, and helping us today against Coach Jim Hoover and his outstanding Walton team."

The game was a spectator's delight and with 3 ½ minutes remaining, we were faced with a difficult decision. Leading 21 to 20 and with the ball on our own sixteen-yard line, it was fourth down and 3 yards to go for a first down. We had not been able to stop the punishing running game of Walton in the second half and did not want to give them another opportunity on offense. I called a time out and spoke to our team in the huddle. The wiser decision was to kick the ball away. Not this time. In my mind, we were not punting and we were going for it as I called the play. As I came off the field, assistant coach Dick Craft and trainer Doug Fry called for the punting team. I said that this play would determine the winner and I had decided to go for the first down. For a few moments before approaching our sidelines, my mind was off somewhere else. I flashed back to my earlier conversation with Fran Angeline and my hope that Joel would be with us today. Deep in my gut and with a quick prayer to Joel, I felt it was necessary to execute the play if we were going to win. Both Dick and Doug asked, "Are you nuts?" I said with a sardonic grin on my face, "I am, and regardless, I'm still going for it." Mike Meck gained 4 yards on a quarterback sneak and we had the first down that we desperately needed.

Clock management took 3 minutes off of the 3 ½ minutes left in the final quarter. We eventually punted but Walton did not have sufficient time to sustain a scoring drive. Dave Zeller said after the game, "Our play means a great deal to the coaches, to the Stephens family, and to our fans. It's just another step on the long road of what we want to accomplish for Joel. He is helping us, and we are helping ourselves." Cory Kilpatrick, our rugged sophomore starting nose tackle added, "We are playing for some very special intentions. Joel Stephens is our heart and our inspiration." Guard Brian Harkness added, "Even though Joel is no longer on our sidelines, he is still our constant companion." During Joel's entire ordeal, he never felt that the Lord had deserted him. Our players felt the same about Joel, vowing to play hard and always give their best effort. Joel was our light and no one was quite ready to flick off the switch.

Chapter 50

Winners in Defeat

We had started the season playing at the Carrier Dome and our goal was to return there for the final three games of the postseason. Lowville was next up for the Crusaders and we played well and made quick work of the Red Raiders, winning convincingly, 41 to 3. Our record stood at 11 - 0 and a state powerhouse was up next for the team. It was Saturday, November 21, 1998 and the Leroy Oatkan Knights, located on the outskirts of Rochester, New York and former state titleholders were our rivals in this semi-final match up. Since Joel's death seven games ago, we had used the motto, "40 for 4 for 24" which meant forty players, playing hard for four quarters, for No. 24. Even though Joel was no longer physically with us, the Stephens family continued to support the team by attending our games. This was a physical game being hotly contested by two teams that just refused to lose. The seesaw battle was between two evenly matched opponents who played solid defense and delivered numerous jarring hits. With 1:57 seconds left in the game, Leroy scored taking the lead 15-9 and it looked bleak for Notre Dame. On the ensuing kickoff, Luke Whiteker returned the ball to midfield and Dave Noonan added a 22-yard gain putting the ball at Leroy's 28-yard line. It was third down and ten and we went to our bag of tricks in hopes of pulling off a stunning victory. Out of a gadget formation, Mike Meck faked a running play to Dave Noonan and then threw a lateral pass to Sean Hanrahan who was standing close to our sideline. I had almost called this flea flicker with 2 seconds remaining in the first half but opted to save it for a better time. Hanrahan had been our backup quarterback and it was time for him to complete his first pass of the season. As he caught the ball, he quickly wheeled, looking for one of two receivers who were streaking on fly patterns to the end zone. He spotted Jake Fiamingo in the end zone and delivered the ball as quickly as he could find the laces. The ball hung in the air as a Knight linebacker bore down on our end. Jake caught the ball, capping off the play and making the score 15-15 with 50 seconds left in the game. It was evident that many ND followers looked to the roof of the Carrier Dome and held up the No.1 finger. This sign wasn't to say that we were number one, but rather it was a gesture to say, "Joel, we are thinking of you and thank you once again." People had wondered through the state title run whether we would get rattled in pressure situations. After what this team had endured for the past 3 months, the feeling among the group was that we could handle difficult times with a sense of maturity and wisdom. Our kicker, Anthony McDonald, who was the state record holder for extra points, still had to make his kick true for us to win. He had missed an earlier attempt but made amends by kicking a 32-yard field goal, keeping the score to a one touchdown deficit. Jake Fiamingo, our long snapper, our holder, Mike Meck, and Anthony McDonald, all showed nerves of steel. The snap was perfect, the hold was placed securely on the block, and the kick was up and good. We had just beaten the No. 2 ranked team in the state, 16 to 15. We needed Joel's help for one more game. It was scheduled for Friday, November 27, where we played for the state title against a team from Edgemont, New York.

Located upstate from New York City, Edgemont came into the championship game having players committed to play Division I football at Wisconsin, Stanford, and Bucknell University. Each team took each other's best shot for four quarters and the score was tied at 21 at the end of regulation. A few years back and before a tie-breaking system was put in place, both teams would have been declared state champions if deadlocked after four quarters. Neither team on that day deserved to lose. We had the first possession of overtime and scored on a pass from Mike Meck to David Zeller. However, the extra point was blocked. Next was Edgemont's turn. They scored on a ten-yard run by their 6'4", 215 lb. quarterback, Drew Nadler, to tie it once again. Dylan Kushnel kicked the extra-point and heartbreak spread through the ND faithful. The final score was Edgemont 28, Notre Dame 27. To those who watched or listened on the radio, they believed that it was one of the best high school football games ever played by two very classy teams.

This season of tremendous accomplishment had finally ended and the players conducted themselves with the same class that they showed in their previous twelve victories. Joel reached out and inspired others, and maybe, nobody more than the 1998 Crusaders. They showed the same grit and determination that Joel had, right to the very end. They wanted to complete the job they started for Joel but it wasn't meant to be. When history looks back, it will say that Edgemont High School was 1998 Class C State Football Champion. What it should also say is "Champion" next to the proud program from Elmira, New York. Many will remember how ND played for the glory of someone else, and not themselves. They will remember how they rode the arm of a quarterback who was shot just a few short weeks before the start of the season. They will remember a season in which a team didn't fear anything, whether on the field or off. This was because the person to whom they had dedicated their season set the example of how to act when faced with odds that may have been stacked against them. People felt sorry for us but we didn't want that. It wasn't our right to complain because we had a few turf burns and we happened to come up one point short of a state championship. Not after we had just lost a loved one that constantly said he was happy to have cancer and the pain associated with it because it made him feel like he was getting closer to God. It would have been great to win, but that would have been too much like a Hollywood ending or a Walt Disney movie. That's not how real life always plays out.

Because Joel taught us life lessons, we were able to handle it when things didn't go as planned. There was disappointment but no hanging of heads. There was sadness but very few tears. In the locker room after the game, we understood that life does not begin and end with a high school football game. Life will go on whether we won, or lost. We bowed our heads and prayed as we had done in all the other games. The effort to win had become more significant than the victory. It was the recollections from the season and the friendships that were made that will last our lifetime. Joel Stephens exhibited class and dignity throughout his twenty-two years. On this day, he would have been even more proud of the players if that was possible. The scoreboard at the Carrier Dome could never tell the whole story. The season had its ups and downs, adversity and tears, joy and tragedy. It had all the things that prepare someone to become stronger, to make them look at what is truly important and how meaningful life can be when it comes from the heart. Joel taught us that and we are all better for it.

In 2008, the Notre Dame football team once again wanted to do something to honor Joel Stephens. This Crusader football team lacked experience, size, and depth. We did have individuals who decided to comeback from serious injuries the prior year and they made tremendous contributions throughout the season. With all "24" players on our roster pledging to play inspired football, and to stay as healthy as possible, the team would once again don similar #24 wristbands that were worn in 1998 so as to commemorate Joel's death ten years earlier.

At the same time in mid-August, my mother was lying in a hospital bed with brain cancer and with just a few weeks to live. While in her room, I asked my mom if we could wear something on our jerseys to honor her, as well as Joel. This was to raise awareness in the battle to fight cancer. She sternly said, "No" and I asked her "Why?" She told me she was seventy-eight years old and that she had a good life, one with no regrets. She would never change a thing, and that she was at peace. She mentioned that life hadn't cheated her of a rewarding and fulfilling life. She then elaborated how she had been really thinking of Joel over the past year. I surmise that this was probably the length of time she had not been feeling well. There was no mincing or slurring of words during this particular conversation, something that had been an often-occurring happening due to her numerous brain lesions. Josephine D'Aloisio spoke of the few times Joel and myself would visit her, and what an impression he had made on her during those brief stays. Barely audible she said, " He was so respectful and so caring, so compassionate. I'm so sorry that Joel was the one who was denied a long life, and it was those who hadn't met him that were truly cheated of that special opportunity."

Once again, dedicating the season to the memory of Joel, the Crusaders progressed through the season. They achieved consistency in their play that led to an unforeseen success. Like Joel, being resilient, spirited, gritty, and with a faith and determination to excel, they became a team many loved to watch and follow. To those of us who knew Joel, he taught us to seek happiness in daily routines and always remember to embrace it whenever possible. Like the 1998 team, the 2008 team did this well. Un-noticed for the first half of the season, Notre Dame went on to beat the #10, #5, and #3 ranked teams in the state before eventually losing in the states to the champion, Southwestern High School from Buffalo, New York. It was evident as well as ironic to many that the two times Notre Dame High School went to the state championships; they were wearing the blue and orange #24 wristbands.

My mom passed away that September and Joel's grandfather, Emmitt soon after. It was tough on both families but I couldn't help reflecting back when Joel mentioned to me after finishing one of his cancer treatments, "Instead of thinking of all my problems, I would much rather direct my focus to all of my blessings."

Chapter 51

Special Visitors

For the next several months, awards and tributes came to the team and to many of the players. We had deserving stars named to every all-league and all-state team, with Mike Meck being chosen as the Player of the Year. Anonymous businessmen from the area donated money to purchase team jackets, honoring us with something to commemorate the example the players and coaches had set for the community. On these coats was embroidered, "Notre Dame High School, Class C State Finalists." Underneath this heading was a football. Inside the football was an orange number 24, keeping Joel Stephens close to our hearts.

It was Sunday, February 12, 1999 when I got a call from Pat Dougherty. Pat was the Superintendent of the Tioga School District who helped with the school's football program. He was also a close friend of Scot Taylor, the former assistant football coach at the same school. Scot asked Pat to make a call because he and his wife, Amy had to make the single most difficult decision they would ever be faced with as parents. A few days earlier, Amy had been in a car accident with her three children. There were numerous broken bones, cuts, and bruises. Once Amy had collected herself from the crash, she immediately tended to her children. Glancing at her two-year-old daughter, Alexandra, in the back car seat, all seemed to be fine, and she looked uninjured. However, after a very short time, she began to turn blue. Alexandra's breathing had stopped and it was later discovered by the medical staff that she had sustained a terrible brain injury. At the scene, this beautiful little angel was administered CPR and later placed on a ventilator. It was determined by specialists that she had no brain activity and the artificial breathing machine was the only thing keeping her alive.

People sometimes confuse brain death with brain injuries. Declaration of brain death requires non-subjective fulfillment of several criteria with the consensus of three doctors making the final decision. If brain death is determined, the doctors are not obligated to continue life support even if the family requests it. The required number of doctors on the hospital staff declared Alexandra brain dead. Keeping Alexandra on the breathing machine was never an option for Amy and Scot. I am sure that if Alexandra was suffering from a brain injury, or in a comatose or vegetative state, the Taylors would have continued life support and exhausted every attempt at keeping hope alive for their precious daughter. What they faced at that time was the difficult decision to either be with their youngest child when the ventilator was removed, or whether to say their good-byes before she was prepped for the operating room where she would donate her organs. During our conversation, Pat Dougherty asked me if I could inform the Notre Dame High School community and have them pray that the Lord guide Scot and his family in their decision. He mentioned that Scot would explain everything to me at a later date. The Taylor's are a caring and faith-rich Catholic family. When presented with the options by the doctors, they decided the best possible scenario was to help others and give the precious gift of life in Alexandra's memory.

It must be remembered that Scot was the coach who had made an off-the-cuff remark about Joel after our game against Tioga in 1994, putting us both on unfriendly speaking terms. Even though we knew each other only on a professional basis and I was still upset about his prior comments, my opinion of him changed when Joel died. Scot sent flowers to the Stephens family and explained that I misinterpreted his comment and we returned to speaking to each other on better terms. What really impressed Joel's parents and me was that Scot attended Joel's wake and waited in line for hours to pay his respects. I noticed Scot entering the hall where Joel was being shown. He was now the head coach of the Tioga football team and I knew that he had an important game that evening. If he stayed in the line of people paying their last respects, he wasn't going to make it to the game on time, if he made it at all. I went to escort him to the front so he could be introduced to Ron and Joyce Stephens, and then he could be on his way. He respectfully refused this favor and simply wished to be treated like everyone else who was waiting in line. Then in a terrible twist of fate, the car accident involving the Taylors had reversed the circumstances and it was our turn to pay respects to Alexandra.

Our coaching staff sent flowers and attended Alexandra's wake. We slowly moved in the long line outside in the cold weather, eventually entering the funeral parlor. With home movies of Alexandra's childhood being shown on the walls, we finally reached the little casket that held this miniature angel. Coaches can have big egos, but they also have a close-knit fraternity that brings the staunchest opponents together during a crisis. As our group approached Alexandra, I bent over and placed one of Joel's angels holding the blue, orange, and gold ribbons that our team wore during the 1998 football season on her heart. This was extremely difficult for a few reasons. Seeing Alexandra's jubilance and enthusiasm on the videos, and then looking at her quietly laying in her casket of white silk just was so sad. Also, seeing someone so young, so beautiful, so angelic and without a mark on her face naturally brought back thoughts of Joel.

When we got to the grieving family to express our condolences, Scot pulled me aside and told me of a vision that he had had before the fatal accident, and why he had asked Pat Dougherty to call me. An apparition appeared to him two weeks prior to the accident suggesting that he begin praying the rosary. As Scot continued to explain, one of the vague figures appeared to be the Blessed Mary with the figure at her side strongly resembling Joel. Scot had never prayed the "rosary" before this sighting, but now he was relying very heavily on the power of this prayer to bring comfort to him and his family. Scot said he wanted us to know that his family was strong and at peace with their decision, and that they were appreciative of all our prayers. He also reassured us that Alexandra and Joel were together, that they were fine, and that they were with some caring and exclusive company. I told Scot that in respect to Alexandra and Joel, we had to remember not what was taken, but rather what the Lord had given to us. He nodded his agreement as we hugged and said good bye.

Chapter 52

Joel Continues to Help Those Who Ask

In November of 2008 and ten years after Joel's death, Tom Hughes, the same gentleman that was involved with the Gatorade award for Joel called me from his New Jersey home and asked if the Notre Dame football team would pray for his son Troy. Troy was thirteen-years-old, played Pop Warner football and was the captain of his team. In August, he received a concussion and when the headache would not subside after a week, his parents scheduled him to see another doctor for further evaluations and to have a scan of his brain. The concussion was no longer the problem. This doctor found something else more alarming. Troy's brain was swelling due to a tumor and the blood was not circulating properly. With this additional fluid, the brain was now being pushed tighter to his skull causing major pain and discomfort. It was also compressing his spinal cord. This new diagnosis was a major catastrophe waiting to happen to anyone, let alone to an active, young football player. According to his doctors, Troy had been very lucky because it was suspected that he had been playing with this unnoticed condition for at least two years. These same doctors said that God must have been watching over and keeping him from sustaining a life threatening injury. After a couple of weeks of CAT scans, MRI's, second opinions, and additional tests, it was determined that Troy would need major surgery in an attempt to remove the tumor and alleviate what was causing this added pressure in his head. Wanting to support our friends during this traumatic time, Jayne, the players, and I added Troy and the entire Hughes family to our prayer list and prayed for Joel to intercede on Troy's behalf. On December 29, 2008, Troy entered Morgan Stanley Children's Hospital in New York City for brain surgery. Jayne and I decided to send something to Troy letting him know that we had been thinking of him. We contemplated a ND football jersey or a hat. We finally agreed to send one of Joel's wristbands, similar to the one our football teams wore in 1998 and in 2008 to honor and remember Joel. We felt that this would have special meaning to Troy and to his dad. In some spiritual and unexplainable manner, maybe it could serve to assist the Hughes in their hopes of getting Troy through this very trying ordeal and major surgery. Tom called us after the operation to thank us for our concern and prayers, and to let us know that they worked. The surgery went well and Troy was released a week later. One of the side effects of the operation was that Troy would grow very tired and he would have very limited strength and energy for several months. Troy received our gift and his father explained the story of Joel and the meaning of the wristband. Troy was a very good two sport athlete. Besides football, he was also a gifted basketball player but because of his misfortune, was unable to participate in regular games until the following season. Becoming bored and restless, Troy decided to enter a number of free throw shooting contests throughout New Jersey and in the New York City area. As just about any normal thirteen-year-old would be, Troy wanted to get going and become an active participant as soon as possible. He asked his father to register him for an elite shooting contest to be held in Jersey City on January 9, 2009. This was just a few days after his release from the hospital. Troy's goal was always to be a professional football player, but his condition and the head surgery may have put an end to that dream. Tom thought the experience of the shooting contest might be a bit soon and with a little too much pressure for someone recently having major surgery. The father didn't want to deny his son the opportunity, but he also was concerned that Troy, recently facing the disappointment of never playing football again, might also have to face the disappointment of not shooting well from being too tired. They talked it through and decided they would give it a try. Both arrived at the gym around 5:00 p.m. and father and son were informed that the tournament schedule had been modified. As the evening dragged on, the wear and tear was taking its toll on the thirteen year old, and he was running out of gas. Troy was sitting in the bleachers, eyes closed, resting, and wearing a sweat suit and a stocking cap. The cap temporarily hid the scars on his shaved head from the hundreds that were crowded into the gym. Tom offered his son the opportunity to go home and to enter another contest when he would be feeling better. Troy refused to give up. It was now 9:30 p.m. when Troy's named was called over the loud speaker, telling him that he should assume his place at the assigned foul line. Troy took off his coat and cap, said he would be fine, tapped something on his wrist and proceeded to the court. Standing at the "charity stripe," exhausted and with a hairless head bearing the stitches of a recuperating patient, Troy began to shoot, each time reaching down and touching his wrist before launching another masterful and pure free throw towards its target. Tom moved his seat to see what his son was faithfully touching after every arching shot when he spotted the blue and orange wristband with the #24 stitched into it. This was our team's gift to Troy and he put it to good use. Troy shot a perfect 25 for 25, something he had never done before and won the contest that was held in the Mecca of high school basketball. Joel's memento not only kept Troy's hand free from perspiration, it served to inspire a fellow athlete who less than a month earlier, did not know if he would even be alive. By now, word had spread throughout the gym of the spirit, nerve, and gallantry of this young man who had defied the odds of his operation and was putting on a dazzling display of courage and accuracy. As the last shot swished through the net, Troy walked off the court to a thunderous standing ovation. He approached his father, once again touching the wristband and said, " Dad, I couldn't lose. I felt Joel was with me." Troy went on to become the Archdiocesan Regional Foul Shooting Champion of New Jersey.

Chapter 53

Joel's Legacy

In life, you should be careful of your thoughts because your thoughts become your words. Be aware of your words because your words may become your actions. Be watchful of your actions because your actions may become a habit. Monitor your habits because your habits become your character. Be mindful of your character because your character becomes your legacy.

Legacy is defined as something handed down from a predecessor or from the past. Fate took away Joel's life, but it couldn't take away his legacy. Joel left his imprint on many people and in many ways. He was a compassionate crusader for his faith. He showed us that family and friends are treasures to be valued, and he gave them more than he received. It was his giving that made people want to give something back. This was the beginning of Joel's lasting legacy.

It is truly admirable when someone has the courage and character to do the right thing at the appropriate time. That is how Joel was in life and now many wanted to do the same after Joel died. They felt the need to follow his example. Some accepted the challenge and found ways to help others. They understood they might never be able to fully fix a problem but their intent was to at least make it better, even if only in a small way. That is why many took up worthy causes to give something back and to keep Joel's memory alive.

People still remember Joel and thank him for helping them to become caring citizens in our community. He taught us how to focus on the needs and concerns of others. Al Losey, a reporter for the

Elmira *Star-Gazette* who chronicled Joel's high school career, and was Joel's grammar school baseball coach stated, "No one could ever do Joel justice for everything he gave and everything he represented."

At his parents' request, Notre Dame High School began a fund to honor Joel. The school's principal, Sr. Walter, commented, "The school meant a lot to his parents, and Joel meant a lot to us. Donations have been coming in from all over the country." One of the donations immediately following Joel's death came from fellow high school baseball rival and friend, Matt Burch of Thomas A. Edison in Elmira Heights, New York. In 1998, Matt was drafted out of Virginia Commonwealth University in the first round of the amateur draft by the Kansas City Royals. Matt had just signed a seven-figure contract and made a generous donation to Joel's Fund. Along with the check, he sent a brief note for me to glance at the check number. It just happened to be Check # 24. That money has been used to fund academic scholarships for deserving students at the school. Baltimore Orioles Director of Scouting Gary Nickels stated with his personal donation, "I feel I am a better person for having known Joel and I hope to convey his enthusiasm and zest to those I meet in the future."

Organized in the fall of 1999, the Frederick Keys baseball team created the Joel Stephens Memorial Fund through the Community Foundation of Frederick County, Maryland. This fund created "Joel's Kids" (www.joel'skids.org) which provides help to non-profit groups serving the youth of Frederick County who are 22 years of age and younger. In the same year, the Mansfield Cancer Relay for Life was named in Joel's honor.

In June of 1999, I was asked to speak at the Ernie Davis Awards Banquet attended by over 500 people. Joel was named along with former NFL quarterback Doug Flutie as the Ernie Davis Humanitarian Award Winners for 1999. This honor was presented at the Corning Museum of Glass by the Ernie Davis Committee and given to the two recipients for their caring efforts that touched the lives of so many people across the country. Past winners include NBA All-Star Dikembe Mutumbo, NFL Hall of Fame great John Mackey, fashion designer and Elmira native Tommy Hilfiger, and Syracuse University coaches Paul Pasqualoni and Jim Boeheim.

Another tribute to Joel occurs on the Fourth of July weekend. For the past ten years, Mansfield University Public Relations Director Terry Day, Mansfield University Sports Information Director Steve McClosky, and former summer baseball league coach and friend of Joel, Bill Steele, have run the "Joel Stephens For The Love Of The Game Invitational Wooden Bat Tournament." This event draws teams from Canada to Florida and from Long Island to the Mississippi River. The tournament was established to raise money for the needs of families battling cancer and other worthwhile, charitable groups who deal with the ill or disadvantaged youth of the region. Ron Stephens said, "If Joel were alive today, these are exactly the types of projects he would want us to help with, and we are pleased and honored to do it in his name."

One of the highest honors presented yearly at the Notre Dame High School All Sports Banquet is the "Joel Andrew Stephens 5 C Award." This is a monetary gift for the recipients in order to cover the cost of books and other supplies needed at college. It is awarded to a deserving senior female and male athlete who exemplify the same qualities as Joel Stephens. The 5 Cs are Christianity, Courage, Character, Compassion, and Commitment, both on and off the athletic fields.

The Elmira All Sports Boosters, in conjunction with the Elmira *Star-Gazette* established the Joel Stephens Outstanding Football / Citizen Award presented alongside the Ernie Davis Award at the Annual All Twin-Tiers Thirty-Three Football Banquet in their circulation area. The Ernie Davis Award goes to the best football player in the metro Elmira area, while the Joel Stephens Award is bestowed on an outstanding football player / citizen in the Southern Tier of New York and the Northern Tier of Pennsylvania.

At The Arnot Mall in Horseheads, New York, the five area high schools rent space to house their Hall of Fame with memorabilia of their elite athletes and their championship athletic teams for people to view. The five schools are: Elmira Free Academy High School, Elmira Southside High School, Horseheads High School, Notre Dame High School, and Thomas Edison High School. In this room are seven large display cases, one for each school that is updated on a quarterly basis. The remaining two cases are permanent exhibits, one reserved exclusively for Ernie Davis and the other for Joel Stephens. They contain newspaper clippings, photos, autographs, and equipment of the two most inspiring athletes of our area.

Many of Joel's friends in the Elmira area have pooled their talents to organize the Joel Stephens Memorial Golf Tournament held annually at the Corning Country Club, former home of the LPGA Corning Classic. The committee includes Joel's good friends, John and Joe Maio, Chad Keenan, Mike Steed, Matt Manning, Randy Harvey, Luke and Chris Sheehan, Chuck Liberatore, Mike Berrettini, and Jeff Sobkowski. Monies raised from this tournament are used to help non-profit children's organizations. Another goal of this group is to erect a bronze statue of Joel at the Notre Dame High School football stadium. They hope to unveil the monument of Joel Stephens in a memorial park in September of 2010.

In 1999, permission was requested of the Stephens family by Kim Castaldo, manager of Wegman's Superstore in Elmira to display a photo of Joel accompanied by a plaque stating, "Winner of the 1994 Ernie Davis Award – All-Time Leading Rusher for the Twin Tiers." This photo has been displayed for nine years in the café of Wegman's next to a photograph of Ernie Davis winning the Heisman Trophy. This is to remember Joel's ability to influence people with his personal and professional accomplishments. A few blocks away from the store is a fifteen-foot picture of Joel wearing his high school football uniform overlooking another part of downtown Elmira from the second floor of

Roundn' Third restaurant on Water Street. A similar picture of Ernie Davis is also displayed there.

In 2004, Notre Dame High School renovated the school and built a new science wing, new locker rooms, and a new weight room. The Notre Dame Athletic Association purchased the rights to name the weight room the "Joel Stephens Fitness and Exercise Facility."

In 2006, the Williamson School District where Joel attended grammar school and junior high school named their varsity baseball field and outdoor complex the "Joel Stephens Memorial Field."

Christina Bruner Sonsire, a close friend of Joel from high school and record-setting Division I soccer player at Georgetown University, has started organizing the Joel Stephens 2.4 K Cancer Run. The "2.4" is symbolic of Joel's high school number 24.

Because of Joel's consideration for others, he is often mentioned at special occasions. He has been recognized in event programs as an honorary usher in numerous weddings of classmates and friends. Other families who knew him have also named him as honorary pallbearer at funerals. In honor of Joel, my own e-mail address since 1998 has been notredame24@hotmail.com.

To all of us who knew him, there was only one Joel. He let his instincts, his values, and his heart guide him on the athletic field as well as in life. Knowing that he was stricken with a fatal illness at a young age, Lou Gehrig said in his farewell to his fans at Yankee Stadium, "Today, I consider myself the luckiest man on the face of the earth." Had Joel had the opportunity, he would have said the same thing. In my opinion, "lucky" does not apply to Lou Gehrig or Joel Stephens. Rather, it applies to those of us fortunate enough to have met Joel. Years after his death, his influence continues to grow.

Chapter 54

Enduring Memories

In February of 2009, I was asked to speak at a football coaching clinic. At the end of the session, a fellow coach asked me, "What was my greatest victory?" I hedged somewhat and answered to the best of my ability, rattling off some of our more notable wins. From the opposite corner of the auditorium, another colleague asked, "What was your toughest loss?" Without hesitation, my response was "Joel Stephens ... because he still had so much to offer."

Joel lived well and he died well. He had no ill feelings and no regrets. Since his death, I think of him often, and shed tears. They are not tears of sadness, but rather ones of gratitude and happiness, knowing that he has impacted so many people. Sometimes we feel that we are indestructible, but learn differently. It was a hard fight for Joel, but we have come to understand that the birds will sing, waves will roll, and the sun will rise and set. We must understand that as mortals with vulnerabilities, we do not have power over certain circumstances. Like worn stitches on a baseball, we learn that there comes a time when things in life cannot be mended, and we are not in control of our destiny. Many of us will go to our graves asking why tragedies like this happen. Chances are good that we will never get a conclusive answer. To those of us who knew him, Joel taught us to live and to think in the present moment and beyond, never getting caught in the whirlwind of pessimism. We learn to remember and respect the past but always appreciate what we have today and look forward to better tomorrows. The here and now are important. However, Joel would say that it is "Who" put us in the here and now that truly matters. There are instances in life when we wonder if we can endure the pain and heartache of losing a loved one. The sick feeling in our stomachs never completely goes away but it does get better. We persist, putting one step in front of the other because that is what we know we are supposed to do.

Making a contribution to life should not come down to a single moment or event. Contributions are something, either large or small, that touch the lives of other people. Joel's entire life was directed at making contributions to as many people as possible and as many times as possible.

Someone once said that God gives us all talent and that is His gift to us. In return, what we do with this talent is our gift to God. Joel certainly used his talents and served as a true gift to God in a way that would please our Lord.

We are still left to wonder what would have happened if Joel had stayed healthy. Would he have married? Would he have been an All-American at Syracuse or perhaps become a Heisman Trophy winner? Maybe he would have hit for the cycle in a major league baseball game? We will never know because the script on Joel Stephens' life has already been written.

Joel never carried a football in college or played under the lights at Camden Yards.

He did continue to do everything else that was asked of him. He was a heroic example and a professional in the biggest league of all, that of his Christian faith. From the moment you met Joel, you knew he was something very special. Here was a person who saw the silver lining in everything and in everyone. God gave him many avenues to be successful and he took advantage of every opportunity, with his greatest achievement being the way he lived his life. As Scott Potoniak of the Rochester *Democrat and Chronicle* stated, "Joel Stephens made sense of something that made no sense at all." He set the benchmark on how we should behave and treat others. He once said to me, "Coach D, please know that I will always love you and Jayne. I pray that you continue to accomplish some great things, but please try and take care of yourself." Just a short time from his final destination, he was still thinking of others. "For me," he said, "the path I am on will lead to a better place, and I am not afraid." Yes, he is in a better place and in better hands. We must accept that. Joel's voice may have been silenced, but the lessons he taught us have continued. He has made a positive impression on so many in the short time he was here. He made us all believe in a higher power. He helped us believe in the power of prayer, and that no matter what the problem may be, it is just minor in the bigger scheme. The impact of his actions is far greater than anything he could have ever done with a football or with a baseball bat in his hand. Eric Davis commented on hearing of Joel's death, "He was a remarkably strong, young man. It is sad that it has ended this way, but look at the impact he had. His life may have been short, but you can't say it wasn't full."

Anyone could look at Joel and understand the effort he put forth in becoming a person of substance, both inside and out. He had a rock solid foundation that was immovable. He never feared failure, and he never feared leaving this world and entering the afterlife. Years after Joel's death, people still call upon his help for their special intentions. Many feel that he is looking down, watching fervently, praying, and ready to act whenever someone needs help. With rocky roads facing us every day, and mountains to climb, Joel may be even closer to us now.

He energized and resurrected our faith in Jesus and in others. He made the way clear for all to follow. He valued and respected others, never looking for any affirmation in return. Whoever said you have to "give" to "get" must have been talking about Joel. He made his own life demands seem so inconsequential when it came to acknowledging and responding to the needs of others. There is a plaque on the Ernie

Davis monument that reads, "He lived with integrity and died with courage." The same could be said of Joel Stephens.

Al Mallette, a retired Elmira sportswriter, said in his book, *Fifty Years of Glory*, "Joel Stephens was the most heralded athlete to come out of our area since Ernie Davis." I would add that Joel, like Ernie, had been blessed with remarkable talent, good looks, and the ability to dominate a game and opponents. It was the other talents that these two men possessed that separated them from you and me.

When I visit Joel's grave, I can't help but notice the line chiseled into the black granite, "Joel Andrew Stephens. March 15, 1976 – September 30, 1998." In between these two dates is a hyphen. It is all that Joel accomplished in that time span that made him truly remarkable and truly memorable. We continue to cherish the happy memories and we do not want to let his life go unnoticed. Those "Oh yeah, that's what he meant" moments still surface long after his death. It is these moments that make us reflect back to what Joel taught us. He taught us what it takes to be a true champion. His eternal optimism and his belief has become our belief.

Joel was a special gift from God who impressed so many. How could you not be impressed with someone who was about family, about values, about all the things that are good and that matter in the world?

On August 29, 2009 in his eulogy for Senator Ted Kennedy, President Barack Obama stated, "What we can do is to live our lives as best we can with purpose, and love, and joy. We can use each day to show those who are closest to us how much we care about them, and treat others with the kindness and respect that we wish for ourselves.... And we can strive at all costs to make a better world, so that someday, if we are blessed with the chance to look back on our time here, we can know that we spent it well; that we made a difference; that our fleeting presence had a lasting impact on the lives of other human beings." This, too, could be said of Joel Stephens.

5 C Hero

During his life, Joel always gave all he could, the best he could, for as long as he could. You could never ask for more from someone. Even now when I sometimes struggle in dealing with his death, I tell myself that God needed a fullback, a strong safety, or a clean-up hitter to complete His dream team. Maybe, just maybe, He needed some help, some role model, someone to show all of us how we are supposed to live.

198

Partial List Of High School Awards And Honors Received by Joel Stephens

Ernie Davis Football Award Winner

All-State First Team Running Back

New York State Class C Football Player of the Year

New York State Circle of Champions Player of the Year

New York State Gatorade Football Player of the Year

Schutt Sports Group Top 100 Football Players in the Country

Eastern Blue Chip High School Football All-American

All Twin-Tiers Football Player of the Year

Section IV Football Player of the Year

Corning Leader Football First Team and Player of the Year

Section IV All-Time Rushing Leader / 3rd in the State

Eastern Magazine Parade High School Football All-American

USA Today High School Football All-American

First Team All Twin-Tiers Basketball

All Southern Trails Conference Basketball First Team

First Team All-State Baseball Player of the Year

Named to USA Top 50 Baseball Team

National Junior Olympic Team Member

Metro Elmira Kiwanis Male Athlete of the Year

5 C Hero

Elmira *Star-Gazette* Regional Male Athlete of the Year

Corning Leader Male Athlete of the Year

Inducted into Notre Dame High School Sports Hall of Fame, 2000

Inducted into Section IV Athletic Hall of Fame, 2009

Joel Stephens High School
Football Rushing Statistics

Single Season Record	223 carries for 1,954 yards
Single Game rushing Record	26 carries for 352 yards
NYS 3rd Leading All-Time Rusher	607 carries for 4,715 yards
Scored	55 touchdowns / 5 in one game
Section IV Rushing Record	4,715 yards
Twin Tiers Rushing Record	4,715 yards

Records and statistics were at the time of Joel's graduation in 1995.

All Twin-Tiers Boosters Joel Andrew Stephens Award Winners

1998	Mike Meck	Notre Dame High School, Elmira, NY
1999	Mike Lisi	Corning West High School, Corning, NY
	Wally Gesford	Athens Area High School, Athens, PA
2000	Matt Dupuis	Corning East High School, Corning, NY
2001	Mike Palienza	Waverly High School, Waverly, NY
	Jordan Van Ort	Corning East High School, Corning, NY
2002	Robert MaGhamez	Towanda High School, Towanda, PA
2003	Kurt Smith	Troy High School, Troy, PA
2004	Nathan Matusick	Corning East High School, Corning, NY
2005	Brad Lantz	Towanda High School, Towanda, PA
	Joe Perez	Corning West High School, Corning, NY
2006	Colin McDonald	Waverly High School, Waverly, NY
	Devon Weed	Troy High School, Troy, PA
2007	Brian Carroll	Corning West High School, Corning, NY
	Mark Kuzma	Waverly High School, Waverly, NY
2008	Austin Rose	Corning West High School, Corning, NY

Notre Dame High School Joel Andrew Stephens 5 C Award Winners

1999	Mike Meck
2000	Josh Wakeman
2001	Chris Alvaro
2002	Patrick Manuel
2003	Colin Sinko
2004	Kellen Dougherty, Micah Norton
2005	Marissa Ruda, Dan Piechocki
2006	Jillian Kreitzer, Zack Manuel, Caleb Norton
2007	Margie McKinery, John Morrison, Greg Schiefen, Chris Wood
2008	Kate Agan, Mallory Lawes, Zack Homerda, Brett Shay
2009	Caley Manuel, Olivia Weeks, Matt Buice, Patrick Sullivan

Made in the USA
Columbia, SC
08 December 2017